Moving
Washington

The First Century of the Washington State Department of Transportation, 1905~2005

Timeline

Moving Washington Timeline

The First Century of the Washington State Department of Transportation, 1905~2005

by Walt Crowley, Kit Oldham & The HistoryLink Staff

Supplemental research and writing by Alyssa Burrows, Cassandra Tate, David Wilma, Charles Hamilton, Alan J. Stein, and Paula Becker

Edited by Priscilla Long
Designed by Marie McCaffrey, Crowley Associates, Inc., assisted by Susan E. Kelly, Luminant Studio

Historical photographs edited by Paul Dorpat
WSDOT archival photographs curated by Cathy Downs and John H. Johnson

Research, writing, and design of this book was funded in part by a grant from the Federal Highway Administration, U.S. Department of Transportation. Printing was sponsored by donors to the WSDOT Centennial Planning Steering Committee, Stan Moon and Dennis Jackson, co-chairs. This book was not printed at public expense.

Special thanks from HistoryLink to Aubrey Davis Jr., Stan Moon, Denny Jackson, Paula Hammond, John Conrad, Joyce Norris, Marilyn Bowman, and Deb Gregory.

Printed in the USA at Litho Craft, Inc., Lynnwood, Washington
First Printing: 2005
A HistoryLink Book
Produced by History Ink/HistoryLink
www.historylink.org
Distributed by the University of Washington Press
www.washington.edu/uwpress
ISBN 0-295-98561-5

To learn more about the history of transportation in Washington,
visit wsdot.wa.gov/centennial and www.historylink.org

HistoryLink

Moving
Washington

The First Century of the Washington State Department of Transportation, 1905~2005

Timeline

By Walt Crowley, Kit Oldham & The HistoryLink Staff

Foreword

In the Middle Ages, when paper and parchment were precious commodities, monks and scribes wrote over older documents to create new books. Later scholars can sometimes decipher the original words and images from these recycled pages, which are called palimpsests.

A modern highway map of Washington state can be read in the same way. It is a palimpsest of transportation corridors — and choices — dating back scores of years, even centuries.

Many of today's busiest freeways and highways overlie routes first discovered and developed by Native Americans, then trod by fur trappers, military and railroad surveyors, homesteaders, entrepreneurs, and by pioneering engineers and road builders. Each generation built on the work of the previous, sometimes following the old trails, sometimes blazing new trails for those to come.

The purpose of this little book is to illuminate these early tracings and the subsequent efforts that have created Washington's transportation system. It focuses on the eventful century since March 13, 1905, when Governor Albert E. Mead signed the law creating the State Highway Board — the direct ancestor of today's Washington State Transportation Commission and Washington State Department of Transportation.

A hundred years may barely register in the great span of human history, but the past century embraces an extraordinary transformation in Washington. When the State Highway Board held its first meeting on April 17, 1905, to allocate $100,000 among a dozen official state roads, Washington had been a state for only 16 years.

Fewer than 1,000 miles of state roads (almost all unpaved outside of cities) served a population of about 600,000. Railroads and private steamships handled most long distance travel and freight, and people got around locally by foot, horse, wagon, streetcar, or bicycle. There were only a few dozen automobiles in the entire state in 1905, and an airplane would not appear in local skies for another five years.

One hundred years later, Washington numbers more than six million people — and an equal number of registered vehicles, which travel more than 55 *billion* miles on our state's streets, roads, and highways every year.

Today, the Washington State Department of Transportation spends more than $2 billion annually for planning, construction, operation, maintenance, and management of key elements of a complex "multimodal" transportation system. This includes direct responsibility for more than 7,000 miles of official state highways (only 9 percent of Washington's road miles, but carrying nearly 60 percent of all traffic), a Washington State Ferries fleet of 28 vessels serving more than 25 million annual riders, 16 emergency landing strips, and special passenger and freight rail services.

The department's responsibilities are only part of a larger system involving federal agencies, city and county governments, transit agencies, port districts, regional councils and planning organizations, Indian tribes, private consultants and contractors, and local communities. Together, all are partners and co-workers in the job of keeping Washington moving.

On May 9, 2005, as this book was nearing completion, Governor Christine Gregoire signed into law a major new "Transportation Partnership" to invest more than $8.5 billion in transportation projects over the next 16 years. New legislation also shifted authority to appoint the Secretary of Transportation from the Transportation Commission to the governor. Thus, transportation history continues to be made in the state of Washington.

We hope you enjoy exploring the roads taken — and some not taken — as Washington's transportation system has evolved, but this book has another aim as well: to help you as a citizen evaluate the alternative routes facing Washington as it navigates the next century. Changing conditions and new technologies will pose unique challenges and lead into uncharted territory, no doubt, but don't be surprised if much of the terrain and many of the choices seem familiar.

Dale Stedman, *Chair*
Washington State Transportation
Commission

Douglas B. MacDonald, *Secretary*
Washington State Department of
Transportation

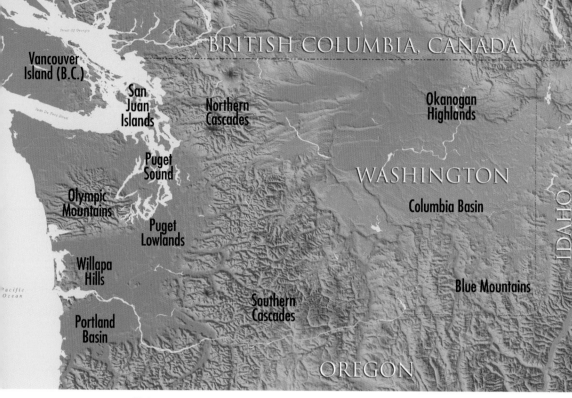

Washington's major physiographical zones. Below: Nez Perce war chief (E. S. Curtis).

Transportation Before Statehood

The contours of modern Washington were shaped by a tectonic collision that began more than 100 million years ago and continues to rattle the state to the present day.

When dinosaurs still roamed the earth, a microcontinent called the Okanogan Terrane rammed North America along the present Idaho border. The grinding of continental and oceanic plates drew additional islands against the new coastline, buckling the land and unleashing scores of volcanoes to create the Cascade Range and, later, the Olympics and Western Washington.

Inland, vast outpourings of lava paved and repaved the basin between the new Cascades and Rocky mountains. Next, colossal glaciers spread southward and then retreated through a succession of Ice Ages. The last of these ended only about 14,000 years ago as the shrinking Vashon Glacier

George Vancouver

sculpted Puget Sound's intricate filigree of fiords. In a final series of cataclysms, melting dams of ice on the Columbia and other rivers broke and released Noah-size floods that sluiced out the Columbia Gorge in a matter of days.

It is likely that human eyes observed this dramatic climax of the last Ice Age. Scientists are still undecided as to precisely when and whence North America's first human residents arrived, but most support the idea that at least some crossed a land bridge between Siberia and Alaska and then made their way southward. The fossil remains of Marmes Man and Kennewick Man confirm the presence of people in Eastern Washington at least 10,000 years ago — and some believe they were neither the first nor the last in a series of prehistoric immigrations from Asia.

Spanish explorations.
Below: Salish women on
Puget Sound.

First Commuters

Like their descendents and later arrivals, Washington's first citizens had to adapt to a wide array of environments ranging from rain forests to high deserts isolated from each other by mountains and canyons. Yet the exotic contents of village middens (refuse dumps) and other archeological evidence show that remote tribes and communities traded and communicated within and beyond the region via rivers, estuaries, mountain passes, and trails. Thousands of years later, many of these ancient routes remain major transportation corridors.

West of the Cascades, the Chinook, Makah, Coast Salish, and others became adept sailors, plying Puget Sound and coastal waters in sleek canoes carved from cedar logs, some surpassing 80 feet in length.

Transportation east of the Cascades was revolutionized by the arrival of the state's first Euro-Americans — horses descended from Spanish horses — in the mid-1700s. The Cayuse, Yakama, Nez Perce, and other tribes quickly mastered the novel beasts. Horses and equestrian skills migrated down the Columbia River to the Pacific Ocean and up the Cowlitz River to the Puget Sound basin.

Tribes from east and west of the Cascade Range met and mingled frequently at The Dalles on the Columbia River. The area became a regional trading and cultural center as thousands gathered to barter, swap stories, gamble, and politic. Natives from distant Alaska, California, and the Missouri joined regular congregations, and it is possible that it was here on the Columbia that many heard the first reports of the pale-skinned interlopers beginning to appear by "winged canoe" in the west and, later, on foot from the east.

Commemorative stamp for the Lewis and Clark Bicentennial. Below: the Columbia Rediviva. Bottom: pioneer George W. Bush.

Northwest Passages

Ironically, the Pacific Northwest's first European visitors did not so much seek out the region as seek a way around or through it. The claims of a Greek sailor named Juan de Fuca triggered an international quest for the "Northwest Passage," an imagined marine highway across North America between the Atlantic and Pacific oceans. Such a channel would shorten the long and dangerous voyage around South America's Cape Horn then faced by fragile wooden ships packed with scores, even hundreds of sailors.

The Spanish came first but they did not pursue active colonization despite their charting of the mouth of the Columbia River in 1775. The inadvertent discovery that the pelts of Northwest sea otters were coveted in China lured fur traders from England and the United States. Explorations by Britain's Captain George Vancouver and American trader Robert Gray in 1792 led to competing claims to what became known as Oregon Country.

Lewis and Clark reach the Pacific Ocean at Long Beach on November 15, 1805.

Britain and the U.S. agree to "joint occupancy" of the Pacific Northwest in 1818.

Hudson's Bay Company steamship, *Beaver,* begins operating on Puget Sound in 1836.

George W. Bush and Michael Simmons build the first wagon road in Washington, from Cowlitz Landing (Toledo) to Budd Inlet in 1845.

Great Britain cedes the Pacific Northwest below the 49th parallel to the U.S. on June 15, 1846.

Congress establishes Oregon Territory (including Washington, Idaho, and parts of Montana and Wyoming) in 1848.

President Thomas Jefferson began formulating plans for American control of the Northwest while still negotiating to purchase Spain's former Louisiana territory — some 525 million acres — from a cash-strapped Napoleon for a mere $15 million in 1803. The following year, Jefferson dispatched a "Corps of Discovery" led by Meriwether Lewis and William Clark to find a water route from the Mississippi River to the Pacific Ocean via the

Fort Vancouver, ca. 1850 (UW Libraries Special Collections).

Missouri River and, he hoped, the Columbia. The Rocky Mountains proved more formidable than anticipated and offered no river passage, but Lewis and Clark finally reached the Snake River in 1805. Native Americans guided them down the Snake and the Columbia to their final destination, the Pacific Ocean, where they arrived on November 15, 1805, at Long Beach.

Eastern U.S. fur traders such as John Jacob Astor moved quickly to exploit the region's bounty, as did Britain's Canada-based Hudson's Bay Company (HBC) and North West Company. In the process, they established the region's first post-contact transportation system, which generally followed native trails and water routes to connect remote trading posts and forts. Chinook peoples along the Columbia proved able middlemen for expanding European-Indian trade. An amalgam of their language and other indigenous and European languages became the region's lingua franca.

The North West Company's David Thompson entered Washington via the Pend Oreille River in 1809 and established the Spokane House trading post the following year. In 1811, Astor's Pacific Fur Company built Fort Astoria and lesser posts in the Okanogan and near Spokane, but these were sold to the North West Company during the War of 1812. Six years later, London agreed to a "joint occupancy" of Oregon with the United States.

Manifest Destinies

The Hudson's Bay Company absorbed the North West Company and became the dominant force in Oregon. It built Fort Vancouver in 1825, followed by Fort Nisqually, Puget Sound's first permanent European

The Beaver *on Puget Sound.*

Territory of Washington, 1859–1863.

settlement, in 1833. Three years later, the HBC brought a tiny steamship, the *Beaver*, around the Horn. When she proved underpowered for the Columbia River, the little sidewheeler was transferred to Puget Sound and inland waters, around which she puttered until running aground in 1888.

Despite an overt strategy to "trap out" Oregon, the HBC's forts found themselves beset by more and more American visitors. Capt. Charles Wilkes upped the ante by leading the U.S. Navy's "Exploring Expedition" into Puget Sound in 1841 during the Navy's third global circumnavigation. He began a detailed survey at "Commencement Bay" and named Elliott Bay for one of his crewmen.

By the 1840s enough U.S. citizens had survived the sea passage around Cape Horn or the overland trek from the banks of the Mississippi River to outnumber the British in and around the confluence of the Willamette and Columbia rivers. The first formal proposal for an Oregon Territory was filed in 1838, and rising cries of "54-40 or Fight" — demanding control of the entire Northwest up to the border of Russian America (now Alaska) — threatened to spark another U.S.-British war.

Calmer heads prevailed and Britain ceded its Oregon claims south of the 49th parallel in 1846 (the final division of the San Juan Islands would not be settled until after the "Pig War" of 1859–1872). By then, U.S. citizens in the region had organized their own provisional government. Their numbers were growing by the day.

Wilkes's description of Puget Sound inspired Asa Whitney, a New York merchant in Oriental goods, to make a revolutionary proposal in 1845: The United States should authorize construction of a transcontinental railroad from the Great Lakes to Puget Sound to expedite trade between the East Coast and the Far East. Whitney suggested that it could be funded with gifts of land acquired from Indians along the route. The idea was all the more audacious since the nation's first horse-drawn railroad had been built only 19 years earlier.

Thousands of settlers decided not to wait for Whitney's rails and set out for the West in

Washington becomes its own territory on March 2, 1853, and the Army surveys possible railroad routes across the Cascades.

Lt. John Mullan begins building a 624-mile military road from Fort Walla Walla to Fort Benton, Montana, in 1859.

Daily mail and stagecoach service between Portland and Olympia begins in 1860.

Charles Wilkes

Fort Walla Walla and Nez Perce camp, ca. 1853 (UW Libraries Special Collections).

wagon trains on the Oregon Trail or by ship around the Horn. The migration swelled after gold was discovered in California in 1848, but the newly created Territory of Oregon (initially including Washington, Idaho, and portions of Montana and Wyoming) attracted a different kind of "prospector": missionaries, farmers, and would-be city builders.

The Other Columbia

Not everyone felt welcome. Upon his arrival in Oregon in 1844, one George W. Bush, son of an African American sailor and an Irish servant, found that the area's self-proclaimed provisional government had barred blacks from owning property. He and companion Michael Simmons, along with their families, headed north along the Cowlitz River to establish a new settlement near Tumwater, beyond the reach of territorial busybodies. In the process, they built the future state of Washington's first recognized road, from Cowlitz Landing (now Toledo) to Budd Inlet.

More settlers followed after 1850, when Congress passed the Donation Land Claims Act granting 320 acres of land to any U.S. citizen (640 acres to any married couple) who staked a claim in Oregon Territory and worked it for five years. As the non-Indian population of "North Oregon" above the Columbia River passed 1,000, pressure increased on the territorial government for services or separation.

Oregon's government responded in 1852 by authorizing the first official road north of the Columbia: "Byrd's Mill Road," between Fort Steilacoom and present-day Puyallup. The following year, Congress appropriated funds for a military road linking Steilacoom and Walla Walla via the Naches Pass. That same year, private "mudwagons" began to offer regular service between Olympia and the Columbia River and the first American steamer, the *Fairy*, began operating on Puget Sound.

Standard and narrow gauge railways in Seattle, ca. 1880.

Such modest improvements did not satisfy "Columbians" who demanded their own territory. Congress agreed, while changing the jurisdiction's proposed name to avoid confusion with the District of Columbia. On March 2, 1853, President Millard Fillmore formally created the new "Territory of Washington," which then included northern Idaho and western Montana.

Fillmore's successor, Franklin Pierce, tapped a military officer, Isaac Stevens, to govern the new territory. Armed with an ambition inversely proportionate to his slight physical stature, Stevens also took charge of "Indian Affairs" and on his way to his new post in Olympia led one of four surveys seeking the best railroad route across the continent.

Stevens went to work immediately organizing the new government and negotiating treaties with Indian tribes. While some like Chief Seattle accepted their displacement by the swelling tide of immigrants, others rebelled. Despite the bloodshed and unresolved disputes over Native treaty rights that would persist for decades, Stevens accomplished his main mission of opening virtually every part of Washington to exploitation and settlement.

Congress authorizes construction of the Northern Pacific Railroad and the first telegraph line reaches Seattle in 1864.

Sternwheeler *Okanogan* becomes the first steamboat to navigate the Columbia River's Celilo Rapids in 1866.

First wagon road is built over Snoqualmie Pass in 1867.

Northern Pacific Railroad names Tacoma as its western terminus in 1873.

Road Work

Road construction was a priority from the first days of Washington Territory, and it was also a responsibility jealously guarded by county governments. When the first session of the Territorial Legislature debated designation of official "territorial roads," a delegate denounced the plan as imposing a potential "vassalage" of debt on counties. The bill passed, but it empowered counties to direct actual construction along the proposed routes. The Legislature also authorized counties to license and regulate ferries on rivers and lakes.

Governor Isaac Stevens

Thus, from the outset, the Territory relied on counties or special road districts to meet its transportation needs. The result was not exactly a coherent system, and the roads themselves were little more than muddy tracks following Indian trails.

The federal government had its own needs, especially in facilitating the movement of troops among its far-flung forts and outposts during the "Indian Wars." The first major new military road was surveyed in 1857 between

Columbia River sternwheeler, 1915. Below: Puget Sound side-wheeler Eliza Anderson, *1884 (UW Libraries Special Collections).*

Steilacoom and Bellingham. Although never completed, it blazed the way for future U.S. Highway 99 and Interstate 5.

Next, future Civil War hero George Pickett built his namesake road around Bellingham Bay. In 1858, work began on a military road between Fort Walla Walla and today's Colville, and in 1859 Lt. John Mullan started laying out a 624-mile route from

Chelan Canyon stagecoach

Walla Walla to Fort Benton, Montana. The last major military road, linking Fort Vancouver and Steilacoom, provided for the first daily mail service between Oregon and Puget Sound, beginning in 1860.

Despite this, news of Abraham Lincoln's election on November 6, 1860, did not reach Seattle until 17 days had passed. By then, the nation was drawing up sides between North and South, free state and slave state, Union and Confederacy.

When Oregon became a state in 1859, additional portions of Idaho, Montana, and Wyoming were temporarily attached to Washington Territory. President Lincoln set these off as separate territories in 1863, establishing the final boundaries for the future state of Washington. The Civil War speeded the laying of telegraph lines across the northern states and territories. As a result, the sad news of Lincoln's assassination reached Seattle within just hours of the event.

Getting On Track

The war rekindled federal interest in construction of a transcontinental railroad. Although strategic considerations placed higher priority on the Central Pacific-Union Pacific route between

Seattle & Walla Walla locomotive. Below: 1891 Northern Pacific advertisement.

Dorsey Baker opens a railroad from Walla Walla to Wallula in 1875.

First bicycle arrives in Seattle on November 14, 1879.

First Northern Pacific trains reach Spokane in 1881 and Seattle in 1884.

Washington's first horse-drawn streetcars begin operating in Seattle in 1884 and convert to electricity in 1889.

Fires destroy downtown Seattle, Ellensburg, and Spokane in 1889.

Washington joins the Union on November 11, 1889.

Sacramento and Omaha, in 1864, Congress chartered construction of a Northern Pacific Railroad (NP) between Lake Superior and Portland, with a final terminus on Puget Sound. As Asa Whitney had recommended nearly 20 years earlier, Congress pledged a 60-mile-wide swath of land along the route to attract a builder and investors. Famed financier Jay Cooke finally took the bait in 1870.

News that the long-awaited Northern Pacific Railroad would begin construction galvanized towns and speculators throughout Washington Territory. Earlier Army surveys had identified a number of potential routes across the eastern plains and through the Cascades, notably the Naches, Chinook, Yakima, and Snoqualmie passes. With the question of the final route open, particularly its ultimate destination on Puget Sound, local communities competed feverishly to curry the NP's favor with bribes of land, money, and anything else not bolted down.

The smart money favored Seattle as the last stop, but "New Tacoma" won the nod on July 14, 1873. A month later, Cooke's financial empire collapsed, plunging the entire nation into a depression. His successors managed to finish a line from Kalama on the Columbia to Tacoma on January 5, 1874, but dreams of a quick transcontinental connection had to be shelved. Local railways — such as the Seattle & Walla Walla (which got only as far as Newcastle's coal mines) and Dr. Dorsey Baker's 30-mile line between Walla Walla and the Columbia — fared better.

The bankrupt Northern Pacific was reorganized in 1881 and its tracks reached Spokane. Former President Ulysses S. Grant hammered the final golden spike at Gold Creek, Montana, on September 8, 1883, but the event was more publicity stunt than milestone, for the line was not yet continuous. Construction and the regional economy stalled again in 1884 and unemployed white workers in Tacoma and Seattle took out their frustration on Chinese immigrants originally imported by the NP to lay its track.

The Northern Pacific reorganized yet again and in 1887 finished the Stampede Pass line from

First Seattle streetcar, 1884.

Pasco to Auburn via Yakima, Ellensburg, and Cle Elum. Meanwhile, the Union Pacific extended its reach northward from San Francisco and ultimately took control of the Oregon & Washington Railroad.

Bonds of Steel

By the end of the 1880s, despite delays and disappointments, some 8,000 miles of steel had gradually knitted the Pacific Northwest together. Given that graded roads were virtually nonexistent beyond most cities, these lines constituted the territory's primary overland conduits for people and goods. For all its faults, the NP cut the travel time between Puget Sound and the Great Lakes from six months to six days.

Rail transportation also offered commuters a welcome escape from mud and dust within cities, where paved or planked streets were still a novelty. The territory's first street railway, Frank Osgood's horse-drawn line on Seattle's 2nd Avenue, began running in 1884. Its success led to lines in other towns. Seattle added its first cable car in 1887, and two years later electric motors replaced "hayburners" on Seattle streetcars. By then, both Lake Washington and Puget Sound swarmed with a "Mosquito Fleet" of steamships and ferries.

Significantly, all of these lines were privately owned and operated, like the railroads and steamship lines that connected Washington Territory with the nation and world. They also enjoyed public subsidies and use of public rights of way ("franchises"), which promoted no small amount of graft. Progressives such as engineers and other members of the rising professional class bridled at these abuses and at the obvious inefficiency of uncoordinated local and interurban transportation networks that were "systems" in name only. Workers became increasingly restless with dangerous job conditions and scanty wages.

Notwithstanding these imperfections, the territory and its major cities enjoyed a growth spurt in the late 1880s. Then disaster struck as fires devastated the downtown districts of Seattle, Ellensburg, and Spokane within a span of two hot, dry summer months in 1889. They would prove blessings in disguise as a new state rose from the ashes.

Left: Early logo. Above: Future U.S. 97, ca. 1910.

1889~1920: On the Road

As the residents of Seattle, Spokane, and Ellensburg set about rebuilding their cities in 1889 — with stone and brick instead of wood — so the citizens of Washington Territory began constructing a new government to win admission to the Union.

The dream of statehood dated back to 1861, but repeated efforts at drafting a constitution had foundered on the shoals of regional and partisan politics. Some argued that Washington should be divided into two states along the crest of the Cascades; others thought it should include the Idaho panhandle. The Territory's bids for statehood were also held hostage to politics in the "other" Washington.

Congress passed enabling legislation for admission of the Dakotas, Montana, and Washington on February 22, 1889. Washington citizens wasted no time. A Constitutional Convention assembled on July 4, 1889, and voters approved

---

Washington state population tops 357,000 in 1890.

Final spike for the Great Northern Railway is driven at Scenic, Washington, on January 3, 1893.

State Legislature designates the Cascade Wagon Road (along the Nooksack River) as the first official "state road" in 1893.

Klondike Gold Rush begins in July 1897, ending the regional depression.

Washington Good Roads Association is established on September 14, 1899.

King County begins operating a ferry service on Lake Washington on March 8, 1900.

Elisha P. Ferry

the final document on October 1. They also elected a Republican governor, Elisha P. Ferry, and rejected amendments to enfranchise women, prohibit alcohol, and relocate the capitol from Olympia. Fulfilling the federal side of the bargain, President Benjamin Harrison welcomed Washington as the 42nd State of the Union on November 11, 1889.

Although pro-business politicians were ascendant during this period, reformers and "Populists" were not without influence. The new state constitution authorized future regulation of railroads and other "common carriers," restricted monopolies and trusts, and banned public gifts or loans to aid private interests. It also excluded the expenditure of state funds on any road unless it crossed a county line or served federal lands. Thus, counties and special "road districts" maintained control of most road construction despite their poor record to date.

Big Wheels

Even within the largest cities, paved roads and streets were relatively rare as the 1890s began. Dirt was gentler on horse hooves and wagon wheels than were brick or cobblestone, and in many areas wooden planking was preferred. Demands for more and better paving arose from an unexpected quarter: "wheelmen," as bicyclists were then called.

The territory's first known bicycle had arrived in Seattle from San Francisco in 1879, and use of the machines quickly spread with the invention of the modern "safety bicycle" in the 1880s. This was no mere fad: Bicycles were faster than feet, cheaper than carriages, and easier to maintain than horses, assuming one had a decent surface to ride on. Muddy streets clotted with horse droppings and crude planks or cobblestones posed major obstacles to bicyclists, who began agitating for "good roads."

The bicycle lobby found a sympathetic ear in Seattle, which laid out more than 20 miles of dedicated bike paths during the 1890s. Bicyclists soon joined forces with frustrated business owners and farmers, who continued to bridle under the Northern Pacific Railroad's monopoly in transporting goods and crops.

The NP's power was also challenged by the construction of Washington's second transcontinental link, the Great Northern Railway. Organized by "Empire Builder"

Tacoma bicycle bridge, ca. 1900.

THE FATHER OF
GOOD ROADS

Samuel Hill (left, 1857–1931)
made Washington his home
for a little more than 30 years,
leaving a legacy of philanthropy,
monuments, and highways.
Born in North Carolina in 1857,
he moved to Minneapolis,
where he became a legal
adversary of railroad magnate
James Hill. The latter was so
impressed he hired Samuel, who
later married the elder Hill's daughter
Mary. Hill moved to Seattle in the 1890s
as his father-in-law's Great Northern
Railway neared completion. He later
made a small fortune in utilities and
investments and spent most of it on
philanthropic causes, traveling the
world to promote peaceful trade and
prosperity — and the use of concrete in
roads and buildings. His most notable
achievements include the state's "Good
Roads" movement, the Peace Arch
at Blaine, and Goldendale's Maryhill
Museum of Art, completed after
Hill's death in 1931. (Top: Maryhill's
Stonehenge. Below: Bothell "Good
Roads Day" rally, 1913.)

James Hill without the benefit of federal
land grants, the Great Northern crossed
the northern United States from Lake
Superior to Puget Sound, at last giving
Seattle a dedicated terminus and fulfilling
Asa Whitney's 1845 vision. The final spike
was driven at Scenic, Washington, on
January 6, 1893, and the first train arrived
in Seattle three days later.

Unfortunately, economics intervened
again as the nation plunged into a deep
depression with the "Panic of 1893."
Hill managed to salvage his empire, but
Washington state stagnated for four years.
Amid the gloom, a small band of bicyclists,
farmers, business leaders, political reformers, and urban visionaries convened in
Seattle on December 28, 1896, to launch a
statewide "Good Roads Movement."

The *Seattle Post-Intelligencer*
lavished coverage on the affair, opining,
"there is nothing that is retarding the

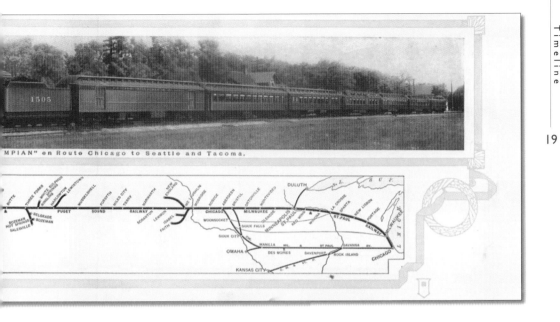

MPIAN" on Route Chicago to Seattle and Tacoma.

growth and development of Washington so much as the lack of good highways." The group vowed to campaign for creation of a "state highway commissioner" to unravel the tangle of county roads, and suggested use of convict labor to expedite road building. Nothing immediate came of the effort, despite the election of a Populist governor, John Rogers, that same year.

The movement was reenergized three years later by the appearance of a new and dynamic leader, Samuel Hill, the son-in-law and former attorney of James Hill as well as his namesake. He invited 100 top political and business leaders to Spokane to lay out a strategy for establishing a state highway department. Only 14 invitees showed up on September 14, 1899, but the number included Seattle's crusading city engineer, Reginald H. Thomson, and influential Orilla farmer Frank Terrace. Sam Hill declared, "Good roads are more than my hobby; they are my religion," as the group formally chartered the Washington Good Roads Association. Its ranks would soon grow with yet another constituency: "motorists."

Milwaukee Road poster, ca. 1910. Below: Seattle's Westlake Avenue, ca. 1910.

First automobile, a Woods Electric, arrives in Washington in July 1900.

Electric interurban trains begin operating between Seattle and Tacoma on September 25, 1902.

Automobile Club of Seattle (later AAA Washington/Inland) organizes on September 23, 1904.

Washington's first automobile with Ralph S. Hopkins at the wheel.

Horseless Carriages

Washington's first automobile arrived in the summer of 1900, with Ralph S. Hopkins at the wheel (more like a tiller, actually). He claimed to have driven his Woods Electric buggy across the continent from Chicago to San Francisco and then up to Seattle, although he and his vehicle hitched more than a few rides on passing trains.

At the time automobiles were regarded as toys for the rich, but improvements in speed and reliability quickly won converts. The phenomenon was captured by Seattle traffic surveys at the beginning and end of 1904: The January survey counted not one automobile at a busy downtown intersection; the December survey noted 14 machines. In between, the state's first car dealer, H. P. Grant, organized the Automobile Club of Seattle (forerunner of AAA Washington/Inland) on September 23, 1904. The following year, the first automobile race was held at the popular Meadows Race Track in Georgetown, south of Seattle, and a car crunched and rattled its way over the Snoqualmie Pass wagon road for the first time.

Meanwhile, the Good Roads Association was stalled by a brief takeover by county officials opposed to an expanded state role in road building. The association reorganized and in 1903 won passage of legislation creating a State Highway Board, hiring a State Highway Commissioner, and appropriating $100,000 for 10 designated routes. Republican Governor

THE FIRST STATE ROADS

The state roads projected by the 1905 Legislature were: 1. King County-Naches; 2. Newport-Orient; 3. Chelan-Skagit; 4. San Poil-Republic; 5. Cowlitz Pass; 6. Water Front; 7. Snoqualmie Pass; 8. Lyle-Washougal; 9. Montesano-Port Angeles; 10. Wenatchee-Johnson Creek; 11. Marblemount-Mill Creek; and 12. Methow-Barron. A 13th road, the "Cascade Mountain Road" between Twisp and Conconully, was authorized in 1907.

Before national and state road numbers were firmly established in the late 1930s and 1940s, highways were better known by common names: the Pacific Coast Highway (U.S. 99), Olympic Loop (U.S. 101), Sunset Highway (roughly I-90), and Inland Empire Highway (eastern Washington). Early road maps also listed several informal "highways," including the Yellowstone Trail, Theodore Roosevelt International Highway, and Evergreen National Highway, which were little more than routes following existing county and state roads.

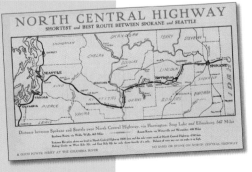

Road construction in Bothell, 1912.

Henry McBride vetoed the bill on the grounds that the State could not afford the expense in an already overextended budget of $2.8 million.

Highway backers regrouped and returned to Olympia two years later. The Legislature overturned McBride's veto by a near-unanimous vote, and a new Republican governor, Albert Mead, signed a law establishing a State Highway Board and the post of State Highway Commissioner on March 13, 1905.

The State Gets Moving

Creation of the Highway Board capped a long and frustrating campaign to develop a coherent and functional state highway system, and it added Washington's name to a growing roster of state road agencies pressing a reluctant federal government to do the same thing on a national scale. As gratifying as the victory was, it was only the first step on a long and steep path.

The new Highway Board, consisting of State Auditor Charles W. Clausen and State Treasurer C. W. Maynard, held its first meeting on April 17, 1905, in Olympia. Its third member had been appointed only two days earlier: State Highway Commissioner Joseph M. Snow, who had served as chief engineer of both Seattle and Spokane County.

Snow was a harsh critic of the counties' track record for state road construction. In his first Biennial Report, he told the Legislature that of the nearly $132,000 in past state road appropriations to counties,

Governor Albert E. Mead signs law for State Highway Board and Commissioner on March 13, 1905. The Legislature appropriates $110,000 and designates 12 state roads.

Highway Commissioner Joseph M. Snow and the Highway Board hold their first meeting on April 17, 1905.

First automobile makes it across Snoqualmie Pass in June 1905.

THE FIRST HIGHWAY COMMISSIONER

Joseph M. Snow (1850–1929) became the first Highway Commissioner in April 1905, one month after the Washington State Legislature created the Highway Board and the commissioner position. He remained in the position until 1909, and then moved on to become Ferry County's Engineer. He died in Spokane in 1929, aged 79.

Snow had come out to Washington Territory from the East Coast with his widowed mother in 1869. He settled on Whidbey Island and taught school for a couple of years until getting contract surveying work with the government in 1870. In 1883, he became Seattle's City Engineer, doing grading work by the waterfront and overseeing the laying of Seattle streets and sewers. After his term expired, R. H. Thomson filled the position and Snow became a land examiner for the Northern Pacific Railway, and after that, County Engineer for Spokane County.

In his 1906 annual report as highway commissioner, Snow recommended that a state highway be built from Blaine to the Columbia River by way of Puget Sound, a north-south highway from the Canadian border to Walla Walla, and an east-west highway across the state. A sharp critic of county road-building programs, Snow wrote, "If one half of the roads funds of the counties was expended in building permanent highways each year, conditions would rapidly improve and the old style of road, 'full of chuck-holes in the summer and a sea of mud in the winter,' would be a thing of the past." (Below: Future I-90, ca. 1910.)

"at least 75 percent of this money has been wasted, there being nothing to show for it in the way of passable roads." For example, only a few miles of the Cascade Wagon Road had been finished since being designated as the first official state road back in 1893. (This planned route for farm produce between Whatcom County's Nooksack River and the Columbia River in Stevens County incorporated a portion of what would become the North Cascades Highway, which was not declared complete until 1972.)

In creating the new board, the Legislature appropriated $100,000 to advance construction of 12 state roads totaling more than 1,000 route miles, and $10,000 for Snow's salary and office expense. Despite his skepticism, Snow was compelled to rely on counties to do the actual work; where possible he strongly advocated the use of convict labor. This was finally undertaken in Okanogan County in 1907, and over the next decade road gangs would be employed on various projects.

Little was actually accomplished during the Highway Board's first two years of existence, due chiefly to foot-dragging by county officials who resented state oversight. The 1907 Legislature renewed funding for "State Aid Roads," for which counties bore half the cost, and "State Roads" fully funded by the state. A total of $232,536 would be spent to build or "improve" (grade or pave) not quite 41 miles of roads in 25 counties over the next two years.

Pressure on the state increased with the rising number of motor vehicles. In 1906, the Automobile Club began installing 500 directional signs on major routes, a responsibility that it continued to undertake until 1945 (the state provided some funding

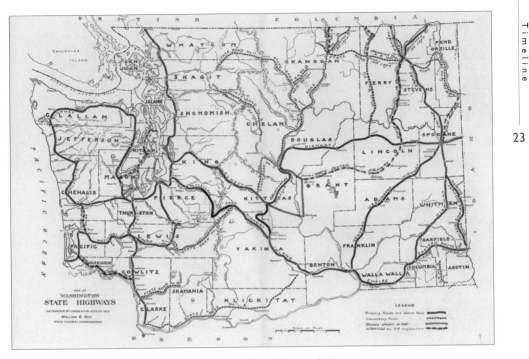

Map of Washington State Highways, 1913.

beginning in 1924). John McLean established one of the nation's first "service stations" in 1907 in Seattle. That same year, Mt. Rainier became the first national park to welcome automobiles through its gates.

The following year, a frustrated Snow reported to the Legislature that in all of Washington, only 125 miles of state roads had been "improved" (often merely with a graded dirt surface), and this included portions running through cities. He estimated that at the current rate of construction and funding, it would require 24 years to build the 1,082 miles of authorized state roads. At Snow's urging, the Legislature raised the State Highway Fund's share of property tax revenues to one mill (one thousandth of each dollar of assessed value). The State made its first direct appropriation for road maintenance by state workers, a job previously performed by the counties, in 1909, and it funded quarries and crusher plants staffed by convicts to supply chipped stone.

This material was used for "macadam" roads, named after their Scottish inventor, John MacAdam. A thin layer of tar, as-

Lincoln Beachey pilots an airship from Portland, Oregon, to Vancouver, Washington, on September 19, 1905.

Automobile Club begins installing directional road signs in 1906, a role it continues to play until 1945 (with funding assistance from the State after 1924).

Electric interurban trains begin operating between Wenatchee and Selah, and what some believe is the nation's first gas station opens in Seattle in 1907.

First highway bridge across the Columbia River opens in Wenatchee on January 20, 1908.

Nation's first transcontinental automobile race ends at Seattle's Alaska-Yukon-Pacific Exposition on June 23, 1909.

The Great Race Over Snoqualmie Pass

The drivers in the 1909 A-Y-P transcontinental car race battled dust, mud, snow, and rain, but Snoqualmie Pass posed their greatest challenge. The first automobiles had crossed the pass just four years before. Even after King, Kittitas, and Yakima counties improved the Snoqualmie Pass road for the race, the route was little more than a wagon road, and it included the Snoqualmie River bed on the west side of the summit. Racers in the Model T Ford that took third place on June 23 (second place winner shown on left) described the ordeal: "We were on the top of the last difficulty. We had pushed through the snow with less trouble than we had expected. We would be in Seattle by four o'clock. When a rock hidden in the mud and snow sprang up to give us one last foul blow. For seven hours we worked on the top of the mountain up among the clouds remedying the trouble that rock had caused. At 5 p.m. we were going again. A half mile over the ties of the new Milwaukee railroad brought us to the down grade and ninety miles from the finish. The rest was easy." A graded road over the pass (below) finally opened in 1915.

North Trunk Highway (future U.S. 99) construction, 1910. Right: Governor Marion Hay.

phalt, or "Warrenite" was often added to create a smoother surface. Many believe that the City of Tukwila's "Macadam Road" was the first in Washington to be built using MacAdam's process.

Planes, Trains, Automobiles

Most of the state's attention in 1909 focused on the Alaska-Yukon-Pacific (A-Y-P) Exposition, its first "world's fair," which opened on June 1st on the new University of Washington campus. That same day, six automobiles departed New York City for Seattle in the nation's first transcontinental car race. Henry Ford seized the opportunity to publicize his new Model T line and entered two cars. Both made it to Seattle and indeed, a "Tin Lizzie" was the first vehicle to cross the finish line 22 days later. However, it was subsequently disqualified for replacing an engine mid-trek. Although the prize went to a Shawmut automobile, Ford had made his point and would establish a Model T assembly plant in Seattle in 1913.

The A-Y-P also gave many Washingtonians their first taste of flight with the demonstration of a primitive Zeppelin (the state's first airship had flown over Vancouver in 1905). Charles Hamilton would demonstrate the first airplane in the state in March 1910. A new age in transportation was clearly dawning, but rail remained the primary means for moving people and goods within and between cities. During the first decade of the twentieth century, James Hill took backdoor control of the Northern Pacific Railroad, giving him an effective monopoly on rail service in Washington.

Henry L. Bowlby

Henry L. Bowlby succeeds Joseph Snow as Highway Commissioner in August 1909.

Charles Hamilton demonstrates the first airplane in Washington in Georgetown, near Seattle, in March 1910.

Governor Marion E. Hay signs "Permanent Highway Act," imposing state control over major highways and levying a one-mill road tax, on March 8, 1911.

William R. White serves as acting Highway Commissioner from March 1911 until succeeded by William J. Roberts in June.

Legislature authorizes public port districts to buy, improve, and manage harbors in 1911.

State engineers begin experimenting with concrete paving in 1912.

William R. Roy becomes Highway Commissioner in December 1913.

William J. Roberts

Railroad investments created public benefits, but progressive and Populist reformers feared Hill's concentrated power. They finally persuaded the Legislature in 1905 to create a State Railroad Commission (now the Utilities and Transportation Commission) to regulate rail services and charges. Soon after, the federal government's new anti-trust laws broke Hill's grip on his Northwest empire.

At the same time, new railroads entered the state. Edward Harriman's Union Pacific Railroad took control of the Oregon & Washington Railroad early in the century, and the new "Milwaukee Road" laid track from St. Paul to Seattle. It crossed Snoqualmie Pass in 1909 on a line later powered by electricity and shared Seattle's "Union Station" with the Oregon & Washington beginning in 1911, giving Washington four direct transcontinental linkages.

Urban and interurban railways were equally vital to the state's development, and equally prone to monopolization. Frank Osgood's successes in Seattle inspired streetcar entrepreneurs in Tacoma, Bellingham, Spokane, and most other cities. Many developers laid streetcar tracks for no other purpose than to promote the sale of outlying "suburban" lots. In the process, their lines defined the relatively dense neighborhoods and compact business districts found in

Dedication of Pacific Highway (U.S. 99) near Olympia, 1915.

the older sections of our state's cities. The capacity of streetcars to move large numbers of urban commuters combined with the invention of safe elevators and steel-frame construction to make today's crowded, highrise downtowns possible. (A century later, the same basic strategy is being followed in the development of denser "urban villages" served by mass transit.)

Similarly, interurban trains linked major cities and their hinterlands, promoting the evolution of regional economies, especially around Puget Sound, which was also served by a "Mosquito Fleet" of private steamers. By the eve of World War I, every major Washington city boasted either an urban or interurban rail system,

William R. Roy

State takes over private bridge between Clarkston and Lewiston, making it Washington's first public interstate bridge, on December 4, 1913.

Port of Seattle launches the *Leschi*, Washington's first ferry designed for motor vehicles, on December 27, 1913.

The Dalles-Celilo Canal on the Columbia River opens on May 5, 1915.

or both, but most were owned by corporate monopolies that skimped on service and maintenance and steadily alienated commuters.

Concrete Progress

The development of the state road system paled in comparison to its railroads. Snow stepped down as Highway Commissioner on August 1, 1909, and was succeeded by Henry L. Bowlby, who complained of the difficulty of building roads to accommodate both automobiles and horse-drawn vehicles. Good Roads advocates rallied in Wenatchee in 1911 and pressed for stronger state control of highway construction to benefit motorists and bicyclists. Progressives also campaigned for public port districts to break monopoly control of urban harbors. The Legislature listened and passed both legislation for public control of ports and the Permanent Highway Act — mandating paved or tarred state roads — while also adding seats on the Highway Board for the governor and for a state Public Service Commissioner.

Bowlby departed that March and was succeeded by William R. White (acting) and then by William J. Roberts. Under Roberts, in 1912 the state conducted its first experiment with concrete paving. It was a radical innovation first demonstrated by Sam Hill, who paved 20 miles of test roadway on his Maryhill estate in 1909. Only Michigan had used concrete for roads prior to Washington.

William R. Roy was named Highway Commissioner in December 1913, in time for the rededication of the private toll-funded Lewiston-Clarkston Bridge as a free, public interstate bridge. The state had intended to pay for the acquisition, but the Attorney General

THE FIRST LIGHT RAIL SYSTEMS

The state's first electric interurban lines linked Seattle with Georgetown and Renton. Growth of these systems attracted the attention of Stone & Webster, the giant utility cartel based in Boston. Through its local agents, chiefly banker Jacob Furth, Stone & Webster quietly bought up most of Seattle's private utilities and streetcar and interurban railways at the end of the nineteenth century and put them under the ultimate control of the Puget Sound Traction Light & Power Company (forerunner of today's Puget Sound Energy).

Puget Sound Traction had a bold vision of building an electric interurban system stretching from Vancouver, Washington, to Vancouver, B.C. The first leg connected Seattle and Tacoma in 1902, and the second reached Everett in 1910. Tracks were laid between Mt. Vernon and Bellingham (building the Chuckanut Drive stretch nearly bankrupted the company) in 1912, but the gap south to Everett was never filled. Instead of trains, the company transferred passengers to new gas-powered "motor coaches" on Pacific Highway, planting the seed of its profitable North Coast regional bus line.

East of the Cascades, private entrepreneurs and the Washington Water Power Company (now the Avista Corporation) financed local and suburban street railways. The Yakima Valley Transportation Company began building a 44-mile line in 1907 and completed it six years later. These lines carried crops and goods as well as passengers. Early morning runs on the Tacoma-Seattle line were called the "Spud Express" after the potatoes they hauled to market.

Volunteers like this Tonasket crew avoided county taxes by working on road projects in the early 1900s.
Below: 1909 Mosquito Fleet steamer promotion.

Governor Ernest Lister dedicates Sunset Highway (now I-90) at Snoqualmie Pass on July 1, 1915.

James Allen becomes Highway Commissioner in March 1916.

William Boeing tests his first airplane in Seattle on June 15, 1916.

President Woodrow Wilson signs Federal Aid Road Act on July 11, 1916.

ruled its bonds illegal, so Asotin County and the State of Idaho shouldered the cost. The Highway Board added the bridge to its "Inland Empire Highway" and assumed the cost of maintenance.

At virtually the same moment on the opposite side of the state, the Port of Seattle launched the new ferry *Leschi*. The little sidewheeler was the state's first ferry designed expressly to carry automobiles and trucks, and she would ply Lake Washington and Puget Sound for many decades to come.

On May 5, 1915, the U.S. Army Corps of Engineers dedicated The Dalles-Celilo Canal, expanding navigation on the upper Columbia. Two months later, on July 1, Governor Ernest Lister dedicated Snoqualmie Pass and an improved "Sunset Highway" between Spokane and Seattle for motor vehicles.

The latter event made headlines, especially in Seattle, whose leaders had long sought the development of Snoqualmie Pass (rival Tacoma favored Naches Pass as the state's primary cross-Cascades route). Native Americans had used the pass for millennia, and the Hudson's Bay Company herded cattle from Eastern Washington over it as early as 1841 (cattle drives continued until 1886). Army Lt. Abiel L. Tinkham had filed a positive report on the route during the railroad and military road surveys of 1852 and 1853.

Washington's first auto ferry, Leschi, *1913.*

Six years later, Seattle pioneers Arthur Denny and David "Doc" Maynard had raised local funds to extend the North Bend road to Snoqualmie Pass, and Territorial Governor William Pickering had championed construction of a road over the pass during the Civil War, but little was actually accomplished. The first wagon did not make it across Snoqualmie Pass until 1865, and a private toll road built in 1883 was chiefly used to move horses and cattle, not vehicles, between east and west.

Interest in the route perked up with the 1909 A-Y-P Exposition in Seattle. Although Sunset Highway was officially designated as a Primary State Highway, King County and localities footed most of the bill to improve it west of the Cascades. Sunset Highway would remain a daunting challenge for man and machine for decades to come.

A New Partner

World war erupted in Europe in 1914. It would have a dramatic impact on transportation in Washington even before America joined the conflict.

Kentucky-born state road engineer James Allen became

From Cobblestone to Concrete

An engineer from ancient Rome would have had no difficulty recognizing the design of most nineteenth-century roads in Washington. In cities, wood planks, cobblestones, or bricks were the most common paving media. Beyond city limits, most roads were little more than dirt trails. In truth, Imperial Rome had far better highways than did Territorial Washington.

The first modern improvement in road building came in the 1800s with "macadam" roads, named for their Scottish inventor, John MacAdam. He designed roads with a top layer of specially crushed angular gravel over courser base layers. His maxim that "no stone larger than will enter a man's mouth should go into a road" created smoother surfaces for wagon wheels. Yet greater smoothness was achieved with the use of coal-based bituminous "binders" and, later, a coating of hot asphalt or other petroleum tar. (Tukwila lays claim to Washington's first macadam road.)

In 1901, American inventor Frederick J. Warren patented the first of several formulas combining asphalt, binders, and concrete in a single application. "Warrenite" was the most popular road surface material in the first decade of the twentieth century.

Faster and heavier motor vehicles needed a more durable surface, and aggregate mixed with "Portland cement" made the grade. Invented in 1824 by John Aspdin and named for an English quarry city, the mixture of burnt lime and clay was not used for concrete roadways until 1891, when it was demonstrated in Ohio.

"Good Roads" advocate Samuel Hill became an ardent champion of Portland cement in 1909 after testing it on his Maryhill estate. Three years later, Washington State engineers built their first Portland cement concrete roads and quickly adopted it as the preferred material for "permanent highways."

The first Portland-Vancouver Columbia River bridge, 1917. Below: State crusher plant on Fidalgo Island.

Washington's fifth Highway Commissioner in March 1916. Four months later, on July 11, President Woodrow Wilson signed the Federal Aid Road Act, providing states with their first significant national funding for highways. Before this, the federal government had been reluctant to invest in the nation's road system, which it had entrusted to the states and counties. Its support was limited to construction of military roads and a small amount of aid to build and maintain designated "post roads" for the movement of mail.

This began to change in 1893, with the establishment of an Office of Road Inquiry

to study national highway needs and run a materials testing laboratory in the U.S. Department of Agriculture. Introduction of "rural free delivery" three years later elevated the importance of post roads in serving smaller communities. In 1905, Congress established the U.S. Forest Service and an expanded Office of Public Roads (reorganized in 1919 as the Bureau of Public Roads). Seven years later, it appropriated the first funds to improve post roads and routes within and serving national parks and forests, but states and localities remained the nation's primary road builders.

The Federal Aid Road Act of 1916 was a giant leap forward, appropriating $75 million over five years (only $5 million in its first year) for "rural post roads" and another $10 million for roads on federal lands, chiefly national forests and parks. Post road funds were allocated by formula to states, and the federal share was capped at 50 percent of total costs, not to exceed $10,000 per mile. Despite these restrictions, State Highway Commissioner Allen wasted no time drafting Washington's first highway grant applications that September.

On February 14, 1917, the Columbia River Interstate Bridge opened between Portland and Vancouver. This toll bridge was sponsored by Clark and Multnomah counties and provided a key link for the evolving Pacific Highway between the Mexican and Canadian borders.

The long-awaited Lake Washington Ship Canal also opened in 1917, while the State adopted its first uniform standards for highway signage and abandoned the use of prison labor to build roads and run quarries and crusher plants.

Washington received its first federal grant in 1917, and spent it paving nearly four miles of Pacific Highway east of Olympia. The state received funding for a total of 14 post road projects and several forest roads before America's entry into World War I on April 6, 1917, temporarily slowed road construction due to the diversion of materials and manpower to the military.

The state's political and social reformers reached the peak of their powers in the second decade of the twentieth century, thanks in large part to the enfranchisement of Washington women in 1910 (a decade before the 19th Amendment to the U.S. Constitution). Women's votes helped create the first port districts in 1911, establish the people's right of direct legislation by initiative in 1912, and prohibit the sale of alcohol in 1914 (five years ahead of the nation).

At the same time, conflicts between labor and management intensified, and World War I and the 1917 Bolshevik Revolution in Russia opened deep political divisions. The war's end in November 1918 left scars and lingering resentments, which flared up most dramatically in Seattle's General Strike in February 1919. On April 1 of that year, Seattle bought its private streetcar system at an inflated $15 million price tag that permanently crippled the municipal railway with debt.

It was a harbinger of future difficulties for street and interurban railways, abetted by the technological revolutions on the ground and in the air that would help give the Roaring Twenties their name.

Clark and Multnomah counties open Columbia River Interstate Bridge on February 14, 1917.

The United States enters World War I on April 6, 1917. The war lasts until November 11, 1918.

U.S. Army Corps of Engineers dedicates Government Locks on Lake Washington Ship Canal on July 4, 1917.

First Highway Districts, each headed by a District Engineer, are established in 1918 (the present boundaries and structure of regional offices are set in 1925).

City of Seattle takes ownership of private streetcar system on April 1, 1919.

First public airstrips are developed in Spokane (Felt's Field) and Seattle (Sand Point) in 1920.

Washington's population tops 1.35 million, and State Highway Board reports that nearly 2,000 miles of designated state roads have been "improved" (graded or surfaced) by 1920.

The State took over responsibility for highway signage from the AAA in 1945.

1921~1940: First Gear

As the Roaring Twenties opened, automobiles, still rare a decade earlier, became increasingly commonplace. Henry Ford's great innovation, mass production, put the Model T within reach of middle-class families. Growth in automobile ownership increased wear and tear on Washington roads and pushed demand for more and better highways. The rising number of drivers reinforced the state's influential Good Roads movement and swelled the ranks of automobile clubs.

By 1921, it was apparent that property tax levies, which had been the primary source of state highway funds, could no longer keep pace with construction and maintenance demands. The Legislature turned to highway users for additional funds. It imposed a driver's license fee of one dollar (50 cents for children driving to school). And it adopted a one-cent-per-gallon tax on gasoline, an innovation that Oregon had pioneered two years before. Both revenue sources had the advantage of automatically generating greater sums as highway use increased. They were

JAMES ALLEN

James Allen, the state's fifth Highway Commissioner and first Highway Engineer, was born on January 24, 1871, in Lexington, Kentucky. Governor Ernest Lister appointed him State Highway Commissioner in 1916 and he became Supervisor of Highways when the state road program was shifted to a new Department of Public Works in 1921. The Highway Department was separated two years later and Allen served as State Highway Engineer until 1925 when newly elected Governor Roland Hartley replaced him.

Allen presided over dramatic expansion in state road building as the first significant federal funds became available in 1917. His plan for the state's primary highway system became a model for many other states in this formative period of road building. Foreseeing the growing speeds of auto travel, he advocated building major roads as straight as possible, in contrast to the winding "scenic" routes then common.

He also added banked "superelevated curves" to compensate for vehicle momentum on highways, among other innovations adopted by other states to improve highway safety. As accidents grew on narrow roads (above), Allen championed 20 feet as the optimal width for two-lane highways, and he called for thicker surfacing at the outer edges of roads than in the center to extend pavement life.

After his death from cancer on April 20, 1934, the Seattle Municipal League praised Allen as "absolutely and inevitably loyal to the public interest and just to all men, and great in that quality of the American Pioneer — the solving of problems by the exercise of a high intelligence and common sense."

STATE OF WASHINGTON
STATE HIGHWAY DEPARTMENT
OLYMPIA, WASH.
MAP OF PACIFIC HIGHWAY
SHOWING
STATUS OF PAVEMENT TO DATE
J. W. HOOVER
STATE HIGHWAY ENGINEER
OCTOBER 15, 1925

LEGEND
PAVEMENT COMPLETED
PAVEMENT UNDER CONSTRUCTION
UNPAVED

34

Blaine Peace Arch ceremony. Below: State team tows car on Snoqualmie Pass.

Peace Arch is dedicated at U.S.-Canadian border in Blaine on September 6, 1921.

Homer Hadley proposes construction of a floating concrete bridge across Lake Washington at a meeting of the American Society of Civil Engineers in Seattle on October 1, 1921.

Fairfax Bridge (now James R. O'Farrell Bridge) spanning the Carbon River opens on December 17, 1921.

State undertakes first snow removal services on Cascade mountain passes in the winter of 1922–1923.

Legislature removes highways from the Department of Public Works and puts them under a State Highway Engineer (James Allen) in 1923.

also politically somewhat more palatable than property tax levies, and regular increases followed, with the gas tax rising to two cents per gallon in 1923, three in 1929 and five by 1931.

In the first of a series of organizational changes for the highway department, the 1921 Legislature, as part of a general reshuffling of state agencies, abolished the office of State Highway Commissioner and made the department a division within the Department of Public Works. Highway Commissioner James Allen became Supervisor of the Highway Division, nominally under the authority of Public Works Director E. V. Kuykendall. The Legislature also replaced the Highway Board (which had grown to five members) with a three member Highway Committee (the governor, state auditor, and state treasurer). Highways remained under the Department of Public Works for only two years. The 1923 Legislature placed them in the charge of a State Highway Engineer, a new post that went to Allen.

More enduring 1921 legislation created the state's Highway Patrol. The six motorcycle patrolmen commissioned on September 1 were the forerunners of the Washington State Patrol.

Testing Advances

The Division of Highways got its own Testing Laboratory to evaluate highway construction materials in 1921 when the Legislature appropriated funds for a facility in Olympia. Previously, the department had relied on the City of Seattle Laboratory. Materials Engineer Bailey Tremper and two assistants set up the state's laboratory in abandoned boiler rooms and coal bins in the basement of the Temple of Justice (home of the state Supreme Court) in July 1921. At first the laboratory conducted only physical tests — on cement, sand, gravel, crushed rock, paint, steel reinforcing bars, and other road construction materials — leaving chemical tests to

Pacific Coast Highway (U.S. 99) near Centralia, ca. 1930. Below: Olympic Loop Highway (U.S. 101) dedication, 1931.

the Seattle facility. In early 1924, a new building, equipped for chemical as well as physical tests, was constructed for the Testing Laboratory.

In the field, the highway department began a campaign to remove advertising signs from highway rights of way (it would be several more generations before billboards on private property would be targeted), and this was declared a success by 1922. The following winter the department made its first, not particularly successful, efforts to clear snow from primary highways, using improvised drags and plows. After the department purchased its first snow removal equipment, it had more favorable results in the winter of 1923–1924, but it would be some years before any mountain pass route was kept open all winter.

When 36 miles of paving on Pacific Highway between Toledo and Kalama was completed in October 1923, there was (nearly) continuous pavement from the international border at Blaine to Vancouver, Washington, and on through Oregon and California to Mexico. Car caravans and ceremonies up and down the route celebrated completion of the Canada-Mexico highway. The Peace Arch at Blaine, brainchild of Good Roads leader Sam Hill, which had been dedicated two years earlier, marked the northern terminus.

Bridge engineers were busy, working for the department, counties, and private toll companies. The department and Pierce County constructed the Fairfax (now James R. O'Farrell) Bridge across the Carbon River near Carbonado in 1921. The state's Inland Empire

The Boeing Model 247 revolutionized air travel.

State installs its first standard-dimension steel truss bridge over the Dosewallips in August 1923.

Final 36-mile stretch of Pacific Highway is paved between Kalama and Toledo to complete State Road No. 1 from Vancouver to Blaine in October 1923.

First autos reach summit of Stevens Pass on future SR 2 on November 2, 1923.

Arched bridges spanning the north and south branches of the Hamma Hamma River on U.S 101 open in September 1924.

J. W. Hoover succeeds James Allen as State Highway Engineer on April 1, 1925.

New boundaries are established for six Highway Districts (now Regions) in 1925. (A temporary seventh district guided Puget Sound interstate highway projects from 1957 to 1975).

Highway was carried across the Columbia River between Pasco and Kennewick on a privately operated toll bridge that opened in 1922 (the state purchased it in 1927 and removed the tolls in 1931). On the Olympic Peninsula, the Dosewallips River Bridge opened in 1923 and was followed a year later by twin bridges carrying the Olympic Highway over the north and south branches of the Hamma Hamma River. The Dosewallips Bridge was the first to use a standard-dimension truss design devised by department engineers to make mass production of bridge parts possible. Also in 1923, the East Channel Bridge joined Mercer Island to the eastern shore of Lake Washington.

Suggestions for more dramatic Lake Washington connections were already being floated. Two years earlier, Homer M. Hadley, a young engineer then working for the Seattle School District, first formally proposed a concrete pontoon floating bridge across the deep glacial lake that separates Seattle from its eastern suburbs.

Ups and Downs

Automobiles were not the only transportation mode growing rapidly in the 1920s. Civil aviation, spurred by the availability of surplus military aircraft after World War I, also soared. Washington municipalities responded by opening public landing fields. Spokane's, later named Felt's Field, opened in 1920 and in 1926 was one of the first designated an "air port" by the U.S. Department of Commerce, which had just been given responsibility for regulating civil airways. Vancouver's Pearson Field, on the grounds of Vancouver Barracks,

A bus struggles over Snoqualmie Pass, ca. 1930.

had already seen many aviation firsts when it was named in 1924 for pioneering aviator and Vancouver native son Lt. Alexander Pearson.

King County began developing an airfield at Sand Point in 1920, in hopes that the facility on Lake Washington would become the centerpiece of a Navy base. Congressional opposition to military spending after the war delayed the process but the County's hopes were eventually realized. Even before the Navy officially accepted the site, Sand Point made history in 1924 when U.S. Army airplanes began and ended the first flight around the world there.

While local governments provided airports, the federal government came to the rescue of aircraft builders like William Boeing. In 1925, Congress authorized the Post Office Department to award domestic airmail contracts on designated routes. With increasing numbers of passengers riding "mail planes," these postal franchises encouraged airline industry development much as nineteenth-century government land grants had promoted transcontinental railroads. Boeing turned its Chicago-San Francisco mail contract into United Air Lines and threatened to relocate to Los Angeles unless King County built Boeing Field.

While the automobile and airplane industries were riding high, urban and interurban rail systems, whose rapid expansion earlier in the century had promoted the growth of the state's earliest suburbs, began to decline. With better roads and more cars, street rail ridership dropped. The completion of intercity routes like Pacific Highway allowed "motor stage" (bus) service to compete successfully with interurbans.

Seattle-Everett Interurban

Mosquito Fleet to Black Ball Line

Beginning in the 1850s, steam-powered vessels provided transport between communities of all sizes around Puget Sound. By the 1880s, there were so many steamers plying the waves that they resembled a swarm of mosquitoes, hence the name Mosquito Fleet. All of the vessels were privately owned, some by real estate developers hoping to lure homeowners to vacant lots around the sound.

The Mosquito Fleet had its heyday between the 1880s and the early 1920s, during which time more than 2,500 steamers traveled along regularly scheduled routes. When automobiles became commonplace beginning in the 1910s, many of the steamers were converted to car ferries. By the 1930s, regular passenger-only service had all but disappeared.

Where there was once a multitude of ferry companies on Puget Sound, one now dominated them all — the Puget Sound Navigation Company, also known as the Black Ball Line. When the completion of San Francisco's Golden Gate Bridge in 1935 released a fleet of diesel-electric ferries, Black Ball's purchase of those vessels gave it a near-monopoly as the region's auto carrier. Poor service after World War II led the state to buy the Black Ball Line and found Washington State Ferries in 1951. (Below: Colman Dock, ca. 1915.)

The Seattle-Tacoma line ended service in 1928, although the Seattle-Everett interurban hung on for another decade.

Seattle's municipal street railway struggled with fare revenue insufficient to cover the $833,000 annual debt on the inflated price Seattle had paid for the system. When the City sought to use its general fund to pay off the debt, several citizens sued. The 1922 State Supreme Court decision in *Asia v. Seattle* ruled that state statutes did not permit the City to use general funds to pay the debt or operating costs of a transit system without a public vote. This left Seattle's streetcar system perpetually bankrupt and effectively blocked government funding for public transit for many decades to come. So while general government revenue flowed to highways and aviation, public transit had to pay its own way until the Legislature changed the law four decades later.

Water transport, which remained in private hands, was also evolving as automobile use increased. The 1920s were the last hurrah for the Mosquito Fleet, the private passenger steamers that had been the primary transportation system for Puget Sound communities since the 1850s. The *Virginia V*, today the last Mosquito Fleet survivor, was launched in 1922. Within a decade, many of her sister vessels were removed from service as new highways and auto ferries eliminated the demand for passenger service.

Progress and Politics

As the national highway system grew, the need for a uniform route numbering system became apparent. In 1925, at the urging of the American Association of State Highway Officials, the U.S. Secretary of Agriculture appointed a board composed of members of the Bureau of Public Roads and of various state highway departments to create a numbered system of U.S. highways. The system, with shield-shaped signs bearing even

Private investors built the Longview Bridge in 1930.

numbers on east-west routes and odd numbers on north-south routes, was introduced in 1926 and has remained in use ever since. Washington also began posting state highway numbers in the 1920s, although the Legislature would keep changing the numbering system for some time to come. By 1925 the state had introduced standardized black-on-yellow caution signs similar to those still in use.

Another highway innovation came in 1926, when the Automobile Club of Western Washington began providing emergency road service through a network of contract garages. The next year the Legislature raised the maximum speed limit from 30 to 40 miles per hour, required stop signs at all intersections with primary highways, and provided money for the first use of oil to control dust on highways.

Longtime highway department head James Allen stepped down in 1925. Newly elected Governor Roland H. Hartley, a combative anti-tax conservative, raised concern among highway supporters when he appointed the unknown J. Webster Hoover to replace Allen as State Highway Engineer. Hoover quieted skeptics by proving himself a popular and able administrator. He established the six-district arrangement (with offices in Seattle, Wenatchee, Olympia, Vancouver, Yakima, and Spokane) on which the regional administration of the highway program is still based. Hoover soon ran afoul of the pugnacious Hartley, and was one of several state highway administrators fired in early 1927, evidently because he was not sufficiently supportive of the anti-spending governor's plans to cut highway construction.

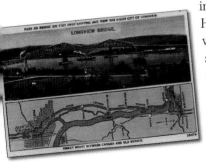

The political fireworks really began after Hartley appointed Samuel J. Humes to replace Hoover on May 1, 1927. Hartley had long sparred with most other statewide elected officials, including State

Federal government establishes uniform system for numbering national highways, including 2,222 miles of roadway in Washington, in 1926.

Automobile Club of Western Washington offers first roadside emergency services in 1926.

State purchases Benton-Franklin Toll Bridge in 1927 (and removes toll four years later).

Legislature orders all state highways to be toll-free and provides for the purchase and management of private toll roads by the Department of Public Works in March 1927. The State also raises the maximum speed limit from 30 m.p.h. to 40 m.p.h., and requires stop signs at intersections with primary state highways.

Motel near the first Vantage Bridge, ca. 1930. Below: Hoh River Bridge dedication, 1931; Columbia River ferry.

Auditor Charles W. Clausen and State Treasurer William G. Potts, who along with the governor comprised the Highway Committee. They refused Hartley's demand to appoint Humes as secretary to the committee (a role traditionally given to the Highway Engineer) and instead selected George McCoy, one of the fired highway employees. In response, Hartley had Humes throw McCoy bodily out of a committee meeting.

The feud over who controlled the committee and its records triggered multiple court cases that led to a brief jailing of Humes for contempt of court, but did not resolve who was in charge. By 1929 the Legislature, undoubtedly tired of the squabbling that endangered the highway program and angered the powerful Good Roads movement, eliminated the conflict by abolishing the Highway Committee and the post of Highway Engineer. The Department of Highways became a code department under a Director of Highways appointed by the governor. Hartley named Humes to the post.

Despite the political distractions and the onset of the Great Depression following the stock market crash in October 1929, the department achieved a number of milestones under Humes, who served until 1933. The first Vantage Bridge across the Columbia River opened in 1927. The following year the Hoquiam River Bridge carrying U.S. Highway 101 across the Hoquiam River

was dedicated in Hoquiam, Grays Harbor County. In 1929, as the Great Northern Railway finished its eight-mile railroad tunnel at Stevens Pass, the department rerouted the Stevens Pass highway through Tumwater Canyon in the first major state project on a road originally built with county and private funds.

The opening of a 25-mile section of Highway 101 in October 1930 cut the driving distance between Aberdeen and Willapa Bay from 119 miles to 28. The following August, a two-day celebration marked completion of the 330-mile Olympic Loop Highway that opened up large areas of the Olympic Peninsula. The George Washington Memorial (Aurora Avenue) Bridge carrying Highway 99 over Seattle's Lake Union and the final paving of Sunset Highway between Seattle and Snoqualmie Pass were completed in 1932. Private bridge companies continued to provide important infrastructure as the Longview Bridge Company opened the Longview (later Lewis and Clark) Bridge over the Columbia River from Longview to Rainier, Oregon, in 1930.

Public Works

As the Depression deepened, the highway department became a prominent source of relief work for the rapidly mounting numbers of unemployed workers. Beginning in the winter of 1931–1932, the department used unspent balances in highway appropriation funds to hire

LACEY V. MURROW

Lacey Van Buren Murrow was born in North Carolina in 1904. He was older brother to broadcast journalist Edward R. Murrow. The family moved to Skagit County around 1909. Murrow first worked for the department cutting brush on highways while studying at Washington State College (now University).

He took a fulltime position after graduation and soon became District Engineer for the Spokane District. On March 20, 1933, Murrow was appointed Director of Highways at the depth of the Depression. Despite a slight decline in construction, Murrow supervised completion of such projects as the state's first controlled access highway, roads for Grand Coulee Dam, and many significant bridges, as well as development of a new highway code.

Murrow is most famous for approving Homer Hadley's idea for a concrete pontoon floating bridge to connect Mercer Island with Seattle across Lake Washington. He oversaw its opening shortly before leaving office for military duty in 1940.

A second lieutenant in the Army Reserve, Murrow served with the Second Air Force during World War II and remained in the military after the war, rising to the rank of brigadier general and receiving numerous awards. Murrow retired from the Air Force in 1953 and remained active in transportation until his suicide in 1966. The next year the Lake Washington floating bridge was renamed the Lacey V. Murrow Memorial Bridge. (Below: Murrow, in trench coat, and dignitaries at floating bridge site in 1940.)

Aurora Bridge, Seattle, Washington

107

Seattle's Aurora Bridge, ca. 1932.

Seattle-Tacoma Interurban makes its last run on December 30, 1928.

Governor Hartley signs legislation establishing the Department of Highways as a separate code department and abolishing the State Highway Committee on March 14, 1929, and later names Humes Director of Highways.

Share values on New York Stock Exchange plummet beginning October 29, 1929, triggering onset of the Great Depression.

Privately owned Longview Bridge (now Lewis and Clark Bridge) opens as the world's longest cantilever bridge on March 29, 1930 (purchased by the state in 1947).

A 25-mile paved stretch of U.S. 101 opens between Willapa Bay and Aberdeen on October 8, 1930.

Mosquito Fleet steamship service between Tacoma and Seattle ends on December 15, 1930.

unemployed workers to install guardrails, improve drainage, and widen shoulders. By 1932, State funds were supplemented by Federal Emergency Highway Funds. State highway contracts were awarded on the basis of the unemployment relief they could provide, with the State maximizing the jobs produced by mandating a minimum wage scale, a 30-hour workweek, and the "maximum amount of hand labor reasonably consistent with economical operation."

The economic crisis brought sweeping political changes in 1932, as the Republicans who had dominated state and national government for years were swept out in a Democratic landslide headed nationally by President Franklin D. Roosevelt and in Washington by Governor Clarence D. Martin and Senator Homer T. Bone. In the same election, Washington voters repealed the state's Prohibition laws. The newly elected Congress soon passed the 21st Amendment, which, when it was ratified in 1933, over-turned federal Prohibition.

Nationally and locally, the newly elected Democrats turned to government programs to put the unemployed to work and to boost the economy. Roosevelt's New Deal administration made spending on public works a top priority. Projects funded by the Public Works Administration (PWA), the Works Progress Administration (WPA), the Civilian Conservation Corps (CCC), and similar agencies transformed the state's transportation infrastructure over the next decade with new and improved streets, highways, bridges, and other facilities such as Seattle's central waterfront seawall and Alaskan Way. Federal grants also paid most of the $171,000 cost of a "semi-permanent" building on the Olympia Capitol Campus, which allowed department staff to escape cramped quarters in the attic of the Insurance Building. They remained in the new "Highway Building" until 1940, when a permanent Transportation Building opened.

With Roosevelt's strong support, Senator Bone won federal funding in 1933 for Bonneville and Grand Coulee dams, the first in

Most cars flunked the state's first safety tests in 1938. Below: Checking truck weight in 1935.

a series of federal dams on the Columbia River, which employed thousands of workers and reshaped Washington by providing inexpensive electricity, making river transport easier, and irrigating the Columbia Basin — but at the expense of the Columbia and Snake rivers' once teeming wild salmon runs. In turn, this led to the establishment of compensatory fish hatcheries on Western rivers.

In 1933, Democrats in the state Legislature, led by freshman state representative (and future U.S. Senator) Warren G. Magnuson, authorized $10 million in emergency relief bonds for construction work. Lacey V. Murrow, the new Director of Highways appointed by Governor Martin to replace Humes, lamented that although little of the money was actually used for highway purposes, the debt was to be repaid out of the gas tax, ending Washington's status as one of a handful of states with no highway indebtedness. The next year a special legislative session authorized the department to build roads connecting Grand Coulee Dam, then under construction, to the state highway system.

A significant portion of federal public works funding in Washington went to airports, in large part to improve what were considered inadequate air defenses. WPA funding provided for construction of airfields at Forks, Colville, and elsewhere around the state, and for improve-

Washington's population nears 1.6 million, and improved state roads outside of cities total 2,980 miles in 1930.

Olympic Loop Highway (U.S. 101) opens on August 26–27, 1931.

Chinook Pass Highway opens to summer traffic on September 13, 1931.

George Washington Memorial Bridge (Aurora Bridge) opens in Seattle on February 22, 1932.

Ike Munson and the North Cascades Highway Route

Ike Munson's 1932 survey of the route now followed by the North Cascades Highway (SR 20) was a family affair. Along with a crew of 25 to 30 surveyors, cooks, and packers, the young District 2 location engineer brought his wife Pearl, 7-year-old daughter Valeria, and 6-year-old son Chuck. The survey party started from Winthrop on June 1 and reached Marblemount in mid-September.

Many possible routes across the North Cascades had been suggested since the 1893 Legislature first designated a road that would have followed the Nooksack River and crossed the mountains north of Mount Baker. Later proposals crossed Cascade and Twisp passes. Munson was asked to explore a route over Washington Pass, then southwest to Cascade Pass and down the Cascade River to Marblemount.

Munson concluded that Washington Pass was viable, but he also investigated a new route from Washington Pass to Marblemount over Rainy Pass and along Granite Creek to the Skagit River. Munson reported that Granite Creek provided a better route and easier construction than Cascade Pass.

The Depression and World War II intervened, but 25 years later the Highway Commission selected Munson's Granite Creek alignment. The decision came after Munson, by then District Engineer for District 2, reprised his 1932 pack trip, leading commissioners over the route. When the North Cascades Highway was finally built along Granite Creek, workers found many of the cedar stakes from Munson's 1932 survey.

ments at existing facilities, including Walla Walla's municipal airport established by city voters in 1929, and Snohomish County's Paine Field. By early 1937, nearly three dozen WPA airport projects were underway across the state.

Washington's airports continued to witness aviation firsts. Four years after Lindbergh's solo transatlantic flight, Clyde Pangborn and Hugh Herndon Jr. completed the first non-stop crossing of the Pacific with a landing at Wenatchee. In 1937, Vancouver's Pearson Field became the terminus for the first non-stop transpolar flight, accomplished by a team of Soviet aviators headed by Valeri Chkalov.

Boeing had by then pioneered the first modern airliner, the Model 247, as well as the B-17 bomber, but federal antitrust officials forced it to dissolve its powerful United Aircraft and Transportation cartel. While Boeing was losing a virtual monopoly, Captain Alexander Peabody and his Puget Sound Navigation Company (PSN) were gaining one. PSN's Black Ball Line automobile ferries, having largely supplanted the passenger-only Mosquito Fleet steamers, dominated Puget Sound's major ferry routes.

Labor strife between the Black Ball Line and its employees was frequent and Peabody faced five separate strikes between 1934 and 1940. The Ferryboat Union's first strike against Black Ball in 1934 coincided with the West Coast Waterfront

Deception Pass Bridge under construction, 1935.

Strike that shut down Seattle and every other major port on the coast for five months.

The waters were calmer in Eastern Washington, where the Department of Highways entered the ferry business for the first time on September 1, 1930, by purchasing the private Keller Ferry and removing its toll. The eight-car cable ferry that crossed the Columbia River at its confluence with the Sanpoil was replaced with a motor-powered ferry as water rose behind Grand Coulee Dam to create Lake Roosevelt.

Building Bridges

Some independent private ferry operations were superseded not by Black Ball but by bridges. The ferry operators did not always go quietly. Bridges over Deception Pass and Canoe Pass to connect Whidbey and Fidalgo islands had been proposed as early as 1907. In 1929, the Legislature authorized funding for a bridge, but Berte Olson, who became the first female ferry captain on Puget Sound in 1921 and with her husband ran the Deception Pass ferry, convinced Governor Hartley to veto the bill. Four years later, bridge legislation again passed, and Governor Martin declined to veto it. Federal relief funds paid for construction of the dramatic bridges rising from the bluffs high above Deception and Canoe passes. They became some of the state's leading tourist attractions from the time they opened in 1935.

Other bridges built around the same time, although not as spectacular, incorporated significant engineering advances.

Ivan "Ike" Munson surveys Washington Pass-Granite Creek route for future North Cascades Highway between June and September 1932.

Yale Bridge (Lewis River Bridge) is built and Rock Island Dam, first on Columbia River, is completed in 1932.

Legislature approves $10 million in emergency relief bonds for public works, funded in part from the gas tax, in early 1933. This is the first bonded debt issued by the state for roads.

With support of President Roosevelt, U.S. Senator Homer T. Bone wins passage of federal funding for Bonneville and Grand Coulee dams in 1933.

Lacey V. Murrow becomes Director of Highways on March 20, 1933.

Highway department establishes first truck-weighing stations in 1933.

Testing for driver's licenses becomes mandatory in 1933.

McMillan Bridge across Puyallup River opens in September 1934.

Deception Pass and Canoe Pass bridges open between Whidbey Island and Fidalgo Island in July 1935.

New Transportation Building, 1940.

The McMillan Bridge across the Puyallup River and Purdy Spit Bridge between Henderson Bay and Burley Lagoon, both in Pierce County, featured unusual concrete designs suggested or created by Homer Hadley. He joined the Portland Cement Association to promote the value of cement in highway construction projects.

Technological advances proceeded in many arenas. The state's first sodium vapor streetlights were installed on a section of Pacific Highway south of Tacoma in the winter of 1935–1936. The previous winter the department made its first regular use of radio communication, installing two-way radiotelephones in Snoqualmie Pass snow removal equipment. To reduce road damage caused by overloaded trucks, the department installed 26 stationary platform truck scales along state highways and provided six traffic control officers with "drive-on loadometers" carried in their cars. The first aerial surveys to plan highway routes were made around the same time.

On-the-ground surveys remained important. One of the more significant in the department's history came in 1932 when young highway location engineer Ivan "Ike" Munson led a survey team into the mountains to find a route over Washington Pass for the North Cascades highway that had been proposed, along somewhat different routes, since the 1890s. Munson not only confirmed the viability of the Washington Pass crossing, but also was the first to suggest the route along Granite Creek that the highway would ultimately follow. Munson went on to become District Engineer for District 2 in Wenatchee and a leading advocate for the North Cascades Highway.

Black Ball ferry *Kalakala* enters service on July 3, 1935.

State's first sodium vapor streetlights are installed on Pacific Highway in south Tacoma in 1935–1936.

Federal Bureau of Reclamation opens Columbia River Bridge at Grand Coulee Dam on January 27, 1936 (the state will take it over in 1959).

Purdy Spit Bridge opens in Pierce County in 1936.

Legislature approves a sweeping new highway code, raises speed limit to 50 m.p.h., and creates new Toll Bridge Authority within the Department of Highways in March 1937.

Lacey V. Murrow, who became Director of Highways at the age of 28, presided over substantial administrative changes. He instituted centralized control of department employees and began keeping complete personnel records. Under Murrow the department conducted a two-year study and prepared a completely revised Highway Code, which was presented to the Legislature in 1935. The legislators did not act on the code that session,

Lake Washington Floating Bridge

instead requesting further study of other states' laws and an analysis of all Washington highway legislation since 1854. Two years later, following the additional study, the Legislature enacted a reworked code proposal with only minor changes.

The 1937 code instituted a new highway numbering system, which remained in place until the current SR numbers were adopted in the 1960s. It rewrote the rules of the road, raising the maximum speed limit to 50 miles per hour, and changed licensing and registration requirements, requiring state vehicle safety inspections for the first time. The new code also created the Washington Toll Bridge Authority, which would issue bonds to fund construction or purchase of bridges, with toll revenues paying off the bond debt.

The same year the code was adopted, four-lane construction was completed on Primary State Highway 1 (U.S. Highway 99) between Olympia and Everett. When vehicle inspections began the next year, they revealed that a majority of vehicles on state roads were operating with serious defects. Nearly two-thirds failed the inspection even though the standards were set to the bare minimum for safe operation. Murrow tried for a positive spin in his report to the Legislature, noting that Seattle, which had begun

FLOATING AN IDEA

The father of Washington's floating bridges, Homer More Hadley was born in Ohio in 1885 and as a young man came west as part of a survey crew. He completed the equivalent of three years of engineering study at the University of Washington, but never took a degree. During World War I, he worked for a concrete ship and barge manufacturer in Philadelphia.

In a 1964 *Seattle Times* interview, Hadley said the idea for a floating pontoon bridge came to him while he was shaving one morning at his home in South Seattle overlooking Lake Washington. He first formally introduced his idea at a meeting of the American Society of Civil Engineers in 1921.

His proposal stirred skepticism and debate in the media, and was nicknamed "Hadley's Folly." Later in 1921, he began working for the Portland Cement Association. He recalled: "From then on, whenever I mentioned my idea, someone would express the fear that it was part of a nefarious plot of the cement companies to desecrate Lake Washington for profit." When construction of the Lake Washington span began in December 1938, Director of Highways Lacey V. Murrow asked Hadley to take a back seat, fearing the flak the department would receive because of Hadley's association with the cement industry.

The Lake Washington Floating Bridge opened on July 2, 1940, and was the largest floating structure in the world at that time. One year after Lacey Murrow died in 1966, the bridge was named for him. Hadley died in 1967, but his naming ceremony would take a little longer. A parallel Interstate 90 bridge across Lake Washington was finished in 1989, but the original sank during reconstruction in 1990, and had to be replaced. UW Mortar Board Alumni began a statewide campaign to rename the 1989 span the Homer M. Hadley Memorial Bridge, and the Washington State Legislature unanimously approved and re-dedicated the bridge as such in July 1993.

inspections a year earlier with a similarly high failure rate, flunked only 35 percent of inspected vehicles in its second year, suggesting that the state pass rate would also rise. By 1939, 97 percent of inspected vehicles were ultimately approved, although many only after improvements were made. With implementation of the new code, traffic fatalities declined from 615 in 1936 to 449 in 1939.

The Toll Bridge Authority (TBA), whose first act was to purchase and operate the privately built Bremerton-East Bremerton toll bridge, embarked on two major construction projects in 1938 — the Lake Washington and Tacoma Narrows bridges. Homer Hadley found Murrow receptive to his proposal for a concrete floating bridge across the lake, and TBA staff verified that the concept was viable. Hadley was not publicly credited with the bridge concept because Murrow feared that his connection to the Cement Association would provide an easy target for bridge opponents. Ultimately Hadley was honored when his name was given to the third Lake Washington floating bridge.

End of the Line

Puget Sound's first era of rail transit came to a close when the Seattle-Everett interurban and the Seattle streetcar system both reached the end of the line. The interurban made its last run in 1939, the same year that Seattle mayor (and future governor) Arthur Langlie obtained an emergency $10 million loan from the federal Reconstruction Finance Corporation to pay off the debt from the city's streetcar system and to replace streetcars with trackless trolleys and buses. The changeover was complete by early 1941 as Seattle became the first city in the country to rely almost entirely on trackless trolleys for public transportation.

The threat of war that had been hanging over Europe became a reality when Germany invaded Poland in September 1939, triggering World War II. The outbreak of war had major impacts on the state and nation even before the United States entered the conflict. Production ramped up at Boeing and at Puget Sound shipyards as the Roosevelt administration increased defense spending and instituted the "Lend-Lease" program to aid the British war effort. New military facilities like McChord Army Air Corps (later Air Force) Base opened, and the first peacetime draft in U.S. history took effect in 1940.

Final paving opens four lanes of traffic on Pacific Highway from Olympia to Everett on September 15, 1937.

State vehicle inspections begin in May 1938. In first checks, 65 percent of tested vehicles fail due to safety defects.

Seattle-Everett interurban railway closes on February 20, 1939.

Tacoma Narrows Bridge opens on July 1, 1940.

Lake Washington Floating Bridge (now Lacey V. Murrow Floating Bridge) opens on July 2, 1940.

Chehalis River Riverside Bridge opens on July 7, 1940.

James A. Davis becomes acting Director of Highways in September 1940, after the U.S. Army calls Lacey Murrow to active duty.

Tacoma Narrows Bridge collapses during windstorm on November 7, 1940.

Washington's population passes 1.7 million in 1940 census.

Murrow, an officer in the Army Reserve, was called to active duty in the Army Air Corps and stepped down in September 1940. James A. Davis took over as acting Director of Highways. Before he left, Murrow was able to celebrate the opening of the Tacoma Narrows Bridge on July 1 and the dedication of the Lake Washington Floating Bridge the next day. The revolutionary structure was renamed for Murrow after his death in 1966.

The Tacoma bridge quickly acquired an unofficial name of its own. Even before it was finished, construction workers dubbed the bridge "Galloping Gertie" because the roadway oscillated in "waves" as high as 10 feet in high wind. Engineers pronounced the bridge safe, but on November 7 it collapsed in a windstorm. The embarrassed department arranged for ferry service across the Narrows — initially using the *Kalakala* — and pursued aerodynamic engineering studies to find the cause and guide design of a replacement bridge. The findings ultimately revolutionized the building of suspension bridges, but the Tacoma Narrows bridge replacement and much else would take a back seat to World War II, which dominated all aspects of life, including transportation, during the first half of the 1940s.

The Kalakala *(upper left) filled in after the Tacoma Narrows Bridge collapsed (below) in 1940.*

STOP PAY TOLL

Floating Bridge toll takers, ca. 1940. Below: WSHC emblem.

1941~1960: Stop and Go

On the eve of war, the massive Grand Coulee Dam was finished ahead of schedule. It came into service on September 28, 1941, greatly increasing the electric power available to the region's growing defense industries. As the water of the Columbia River rose behind the dam to form the vast reservoir that, after the president's death, would be named Lake Roosevelt, the highway department worked to replace roads and bridges that would soon be submerged. In May a new bridge opened to traffic at Kettle Falls, and the Spokane River Bridge at Fort Spokane opened in December, two days before Japan attacked Pearl Harbor.

American entry into the war brought far-reaching changes. At President Roosevelt's request, the maximum speed limit was reduced to 35 miles per hour to conserve vehicles, gasoline, and rubber for the war effort. The department's Traffic Engineering Division conducted regular speed checks to monitor observance of the new limit. Gas rationing was soon introduced, further restricting travel. By the end of

1942, with driving down, spare parts hard to come by, and facing manpower shortages, the department suspended vehicle inspections for the duration of the war.

Burwell Bantz, who became Director of Highways in 1941 and led the department through most of the war years, reported that highway construction was confined largely to military access roads, flight strips, and other projects to aid the war effort. Maintenance work was limited to that necessary to keep highways safe. Bantz had to deal with high turnover and recruiting difficulties as the department's younger employees entered military service and many others left for higher paying jobs in defense work.

51

Life During Wartime

Fear of an attack on Washington's coast ran high after Pearl Harbor. In February 1942, at the urging of elected officials and military authorities, President Roosevelt signed Executive Order 9066 mandating the forced evacuation of Japanese American residents from the West Coast. Nearly 13,000 Washingtonians of Japanese descent were among the 110,000 people, two-thirds of them U.S. citizens, removed from their homes to "internment" camps in the interior of the country.

Another group of Washington residents also lost homes during the war. In early 1943, farmers and other landowners on the dry plains along the Columbia River west of the small towns of White Bluffs, Hanford, and Richland were informed that their property was being condemned for a secret government project. Construction soon began on the Hanford Engineer Works that would produce plutonium for atomic bombs. Along with three nuclear reactors, some 500 support facilities, and a new "government city" at Richland to house 17,500 people, the Hanford project required building 386 miles of roads and 158 miles of railroad.

The thousands of workers and their families who flocked to Hanford from around the country were just part of the flood of newcomers working in the state's booming defense industries. Boeing's aircraft factories, shipyards on Puget Sound and the Columbia River, and military bases around the state all needed workers. Washington, one of the top two states

Legislature creates Highway Advisory Commission in March 1941.

Last Seattle streetcar completes its final run on April 13, 1941, as the city converts to buses and new electric "trackless trolleys."

Columbia River Bridge at Kettle Falls opens on May 3, 1941.

Burwell Bantz is named Director of Highways on July 1, 1941.

Snoqualmie Pass radio operator, 1940s.

First and second Kettle Falls bridges, ca. 1941. Below: President Roosevelt touring Grand Coulee, 1937.

Japan attacks Pearl Harbor on December 7, 1941, and the U.S. formally enters World War II the next day. Gas rationing is soon imposed, maximum speed limits are reduced to 35 m.p.h., and vehicle inspections are suspended for the duration.

President Roosevelt signs Executive Order 9066 relocating Japanese Americans from West Coast on February 19, 1942.

Cameras and binoculars are banned from all ferries in the state on May 30, 1942.

Construction of secret nuclear processing facilities begins at Hanford in March 1943.

Washington State Patrol takes over truck-weighing stations on March 31, 1943.

in the country in war contracts per capita, saw its 1940 population of 1.7 million rise by 250,000 during the war. A significant number of the newcomers were African American. Defense spending accelerated development of aviation facilities that was already underway. More than $100 million went to develop 35 air bases, landing fields, and related projects in Washington. Spokane got the largest share, with $27 million for the Army Air Depot (which became Fairchild Air Force Base in 1951), and another $9 million for Geiger Field. In the Puget Sound area, millions were spent to develop Boeing, Paine, and McChord fields for military use.

As the military took over most existing airports, area officials realized that a new facility was needed for civilian use. In March 1942, the Port of Seattle agreed to the request of the federal Civil Aviation Authority to

GREENING THE DESERT

In 1918, when a small group of Eastern Washington businessmen began promoting a plan to plug the Columbia River with concrete and use the water to irrigate a million acres of desert, it took two days to travel the 90-some miles between Wenatchee and the potential damsite. Today, it's an easy hour and a half on the smooth asphalt of Washington State Routes 28, 17, and 155. This is one small example of the profound changes brought to the Pacific Northwest by the Columbia Basin Project.

The centerpiece of the project is Grand Coulee Dam: 12 million cubic yards of concrete stacked 550 feet high, backing up a 150-mile reservoir, and generating more electricity than any other dam in the United States. Hailed as the "Eighth Wonder of the World" when it was completed in 1941, the dam was already a tourist attraction. More than 300,000 people came to see it in 1940, which put pressure on the highway department to improve the local highways.

As gargantuan as it is, Grand Coulee is only part of a massive irrigation system that includes five other dams, four major storage lakes and numerous smaller ones, more than 2,300 miles of canals, 3,500 miles of drains and ditches, and dozens of pumping plants. The distribution system required more time, money, and engineering skill than the original dam. And it is still only half complete, providing water to a mere 550,000 acres instead of the million originally planned.

When excavation for the dam began in 1933, the only roadways in the area were dirt or gravel, leading to isolated farms and ranches. In January 1934, the Washington Legislature authorized the highway department to build roads connecting the state highway system to the damsite and the five towns that had sprung up around it. The U.S. Bureau of Reclamation (lead agency for the Columbia Basin Project) built most of the roads, bridges, and railroads within the initial project area, but the highway department constructed two steel cantilever bridges over the Columbia, at Kettle Falls and at Fort Spokane, to replace bridges flooded by the dam in 1941.

Work on the irrigation project did not begin until after World War II and continued for decades before being halted by environmental and other concerns. In 1951, when the primary canals and the main pumping plant were completed, the Legislature authorized $5 million for new road construction in the Columbia Basin. One of the primary routes was State Route 155, linking Coulee City with Omak. This highway includes the Columbia River Bridge near the dam, built by the Bureau of Reclamation in 1936 and later turned over to the state. The highways and bridges now bisect a land transformed by the geometry of water — sagebrush and tumbleweed on one side of the canals, squares and circles of lush green on the other.

develop a new regional airport. With encouragement and additional funding from Tacoma and Pierce County, a site in south King County midway between Seattle and Tacoma was chosen for what would become Sea-Tac Airport. The runway was finished in 1944, but even that was temporarily taken over by the Army Air Force to shuttle bombers to the Pacific. It was another few years before the new airport saw significant commercial use.

The wartime election of 1944 set a state record for voter turnout that has yet to be surpassed. President Roosevelt was elected to an unprecedented fourth term but he died in April 1945 and was succeeded by Harry Truman. Warren Magnuson was elected to the U.S. Senate where he would serve six terms and use his increasing clout to obtain vast federal appropriations for highway, bridge, and transit projects across Washington.

Northgate, ca. 1950. Below: Future Sen. Warren G. Magnuson, ca. 1938.

Fellow Democrat Mon Wallgren left a Senate seat to oust Arthur Langlie (temporarily) from the governor's mansion.

Most significant for Washington's transportation future, voters approved the 18th Amendment to the Washington Constitution, which mandated that all revenue from motor vehicle fuel taxes, vehicle license fees, and other revenue intended for highway purposes (not including driver's license fees and motor vehicle excise taxes) be used exclusively for highway purposes, defined to include ferries operated as part of the highway system. The "Good Roads Amendment" was proposed by the Legislature at the request of the influential Good Roads Association. The association and other highway advocates were unhappy that over the past 10 years more than $10 million in gas-tax revenues had gone into the general fund as legislators sought additional revenue to supplement the property tax, which had been capped at 40 mills, and to boost spending during the Depression.

In the voters' pamphlet they argued: "These were highways and streets we paid for, but didn't get! Now you can stop further diversion." Although some legislators had voted against sending the proposal to voters, there was no statement against and no organized opposition, and the amendment won handily. It would

New Federal Aid Highway Act imposes higher design standards on interstate highways in 1944.

Voters approve Amendment 18 to the state constitution, limiting all highway-related revenues, e.g., the gas tax, to highway uses only on November 7, 1944.

Governor Wallgren appoints Clarence Hickey as Director of Highways on January 11, 1945, but he dies suddenly in June. James A. Davis is again named acting director until Clarence Shain succeeds him in October.

Boeing B-29s drop atomic bombs on Hiroshima and Nagasaki on August 6 and 9, 1945, and Japan surrenders on August 14.

later have the apparently unintended consequence of blocking use of gas-tax funds for mass transit and other non-highway transportation improvements.

Governor Wallgren appointed Clarence Hickey to replace Bantz as Director of Highways in January 1945, but Hickey died in June. James Davis served a second time as acting director until the governor named Clarence Shain director in October. By then the war had ended. Germany surrendered in May and Japan followed in August, shortly after Boeing B-29s dropped the first atomic bombs used in war. U.S. 99 was designated a "Blue Star Highway" that same year to honor America's fallen (it had also been designated as Jefferson Davis Memorial Highway in 1939 to honor Davis's service as Secretary of War in the 1850s before he became president of the Confederacy).

Post-War Development

Gas rationing ended soon after the war did and the 35 miles per hour speed limit was lifted. Shain reported that traffic volumes doubled within a month and the accident rate jumped. With drivers back on the road and pent-up demand for new homes and consumer goods released, residential and commercial development took off, much of it in the fast growing suburbs. Bellevue Square opened in 1946 as the first regional suburban shopping center in the Pacific Northwest. It was followed four years later by Northgate Shopping Mall (located north of what was then Seattle's city limit), the nation's first regional shopping center designed as a "mall."

Sea-Tac Airport Terminal, ca. 1950.

For long-distance travel, railroads declined in importance while airline travel steadily increased as did the number of private pilots. The Legislature responded in 1947 with creation of a State Aeronautics Commission to construct emergency landing fields, chiefly in and around the Cascades. The commission eventually expanded its responsibilities to include pilot licensing and flight education certifications.

By 1947, many (though not all) airports that had been taken for military use were returned to local control and commercial use. Geiger Field became the Spokane municipal (later International) airport, while neighboring Fairchild remained a major Air Force base. The Walla Walla field, home to nearly 600 bomber crews during the war, became a municipal airport once more. Snohomish County's Paine Field continued to see both civil and military use, while the military retained exclusive control of McChord Air

First stores in Bellevue Square shopping center open on August 20, 1946.

Legislature authorizes limited-access highways and establishes an Aeronautics Commission in March 1947.

State Toll Bridge Authority purchases Longview Toll Bridge for $2.25 million on December 16, 1947.

First Columbia Basin irrigation water is turned on at Pasco Heights on May 15, 1948.

New Keller Ferry, the *Martha S.,* begins service on Lake Roosevelt on September 9, 1948.

Building the second Vancouver-Portland Interstate Bridge, ca. 1958. Lower right: ferry Martha S., *ca. 2005.*

O. R. Dinsmore becomes acting director in January 1949 and serves until July, when William A. Bugge becomes Director of Highways.

Legislature raises gas tax to 6.5 cents per gallon and establishes a "merit system" for Department of Highways personnel in March 1949.

Lake Washington Floating Bridge tolls end on July 2, 1949.

Governor Arthur Langlie dedicates the first Seattle-Tacoma International Airport terminal on July 9, 1949.

Force Base in Pierce County. As the bombers departed the Seattle-Tacoma International Airport in 1946, commercial use expanded, although it was not until 1949, when the original administration and passenger terminal building was dedicated, that the airport officially added "International" to its name. Moving auto traffic to and from growing airports would soon become a major challenge for highway planners.

In another portent of things to come, the 1947 Legislature passed the state's first law authorizing construction of limited-access highways, making possible safer roads and higher speeds but upsetting roadside business owners. This first law had little practical effect because it did not allow the department to close access on existing highways, which frustrated plans to upgrade Highway 99 and other key routes. At the end of the year, the Toll Bridge Authority purchased the Longview Toll Bridge from its private owners.

The first irrigation water from Columbia Basin Project dams was pumped at a demonstration site in Pasco Heights in May 1948, beginning the transformation of an arid desert into some of the nation's most productive farmland. As the fields bloomed over the following years, the highway department improved Columbia Basin roads, including many built by the federal government as part of the dam projects, and constructed more in order to get the region's new produce to market.

Ironically, the long-awaited irrigation water from the Columbia was soon followed by floods. In late May 1948, one of the most destructive floods in the Columbia's history inundated communities all along the river, bringing transportation to a temporary standstill and wiping out many roads and bridges. The department was still rebuilding when a severe earthquake struck Western Washington the following April, inflicting further damage on the highway system. The 1948 flood helped spur another two decades of dam building on the Columbia for flood control as well as power production and irrigation.

A LONG DRIVE

William Adair Bugge, born in Hadlock, Jefferson County, in 1900, was named Director of Highways in 1949 and held this position for 14 years, streamlining the department's structure and overseeing major road and bridge construction.

In 1949, 52 percent of state roads were rated "deficient." While in office, Bugge reorganized the department, reducing staff and department expenditures. He started a new classification system that prioritized construction on a most-needed basis, and also decentralized operations by leaving contracts and planning to district offices. He administered 3,600 construction contracts, built 4,107 miles of highways, and spent more money than had been spent previously in the combined 44-year history of the highway department.

The planning for Interstate 5 and the Puget Sound Regional Transportation Study began under his watch, as did the first use of computers in the department. He was called "a master of diplomacy," and won three major national awards within one year (1960–1961), also winning the Traffic Engineering Award four years running (1951–1954). He continued in the position until May 21, 1963, when he resigned to take the job of project director in charge of design and construction of the $1.5 billion Bay Area Rapid Transit System (BART) in San Francisco. Bugge died in 1992, and the Hood Canal Floating Bridge now bears his name.

Ferries and Bridges

In September 1948 the highway department launched the *Martha S.*, named for director Clarence Shain's wife, as the new Keller Ferry on Lake Roosevelt, upriver from the Columbia project's Grand Coulee Dam. Within a few years of its launch, the *Martha S.*, which is still in service, was joined in state ownership by the much larger fleet of ferries on Puget Sound.

Labor disputes between the Black Ball Line president, Alexander Peabody, and his union employees, temporarily set aside during World War II, flared again at the end of the decade. In 1947, the Marine Engineers union went on strike in support of their demand for a 40-hour work week, idling Black Ball's 22 ferries and stranding thousands of commuters. Governor Wallgren mediated a settlement, but Captain Peabody shut Black Ball down again a year later after the State refused his request for a 30 percent fare increase.

Puget Sound counties had little alternative but to enter agreements granting Black Ball higher fares. Service resumed, but pressure built for the State to operate its own ferries. Wallgren promised a state ferry system, run by the Toll Bridge Authority (rather than directly managed by the highway department) in order to placate taxpayers east of the mountains who feared diversion of gas-tax revenues. But having made ferries a campaign issue, Wallgren was unable to deliver on his promise.

The ferry mess and other missteps helped former governor Arthur Langlie defeat the man who had beaten him four years earlier. During the campaign Langlie, a moderate Republican who usually supported private enterprise, denounced Peabody and called for the State to run the ferries as a public utility, touting his success in modernizing Seattle's transportation system in 1940.

58

Langlie signed legislation authorizing the State to run a ferry system soon after he took office, but terms were not settled until the end of 1949 for the State to take over most of the company's routes, terminals, and ferries for a total price of $6.8 million. It was 18 more months before the changeover took effect. Langlie also appointed William A. Bugge as Director of Highways.

The 1949 Legislature raised the gas tax and established a special personnel merit system for highway department employees. The increase from five to six-and-a-half cents per gallon was the first for the gas tax since 1931. With construction bonds for the Lake Washington Floating Bridge nearly paid off, tolls were removed in 1949. This spelled the end of almost 70 years of regular Lake Washington ferry service following year.

The Toll Bridge Authority celebrated two major bridge openings in October 1950: the Agate Pass Toll Bridge connecting Bainbridge Island to the Kitsap County mainland, and the second Tacoma Narrows Bridge, replacing the bridge that collapsed in a 1940 windstorm. The latter was the first suspension bridge built in the U.S. since "Galloping Gertie's" collapse. Design Engineer Dexter Smith and Principal Engineer Charles Andrew worked with engineering professors from the University of Washington and California Institute of Technology to incorporate lessons learned

Northgate, the nation's first mall-type shopping center, opens north of Seattle on April 21, 1950.

Ferry *Leschi* completes her last scheduled run on Lake Washington on August 31, 1950.

Agate Pass Bridge between Bainbridge Island and Kitsap Peninsula opens on October 7, 1950.

New highway bridge (named the Sellars Bridge in 2000) opens at Wenatchee on October 8, 1950, and wins national praise.

Replacement Tacoma Narrows Bridge opens on October 14, 1950.

Population of Washington state reaches 2,378,963, and total improved state highway mileage tops 6,270 miles in 1950.

Second Tacoma Narrows Bridge, 1950.

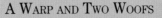

A Warp and Two Woofs

When Washington State Ferries took over operation of the Puget Sound Navigation Company in 1951, it was done with little fanfare. The drawn-out battle over public vs. private ferry operations had been hard fought, and WSF was simply looking forward to smooth sailing with past events in their wake.

Ferry passengers noticed little difference. The boats were the same, the same folks who worked for Black Ball were still on board, and there was very little change to the schedules. But the truly observant noticed one subtle change: the landing call on the whistle was now one long blast followed by a short (a warp and a woof) instead of the traditional Puget Sound ferry call of a long and two shorts.

The new whistle call lasted only a few years, and the "warp and two woofs" was reinstated in 1958 after WSF listened to pleas from maritime historians and ferry workers who argued that tradition must be kept. These folks also convinced the ferry system to continue the tradition of naming new vessels with Indian names, which Black Ball had done for years. Thus, the vessels slated to be named the *Vacation State* and the *Washington State* became the *Klahowya* ("greetings") and the *Tillikum* ("people" or "friends"). Since then, all ferries have been named in keeping with this tradition.

Black Ball Line head Alexander Peabody, the San Mateo, *and Colman Dock, 1930s.*

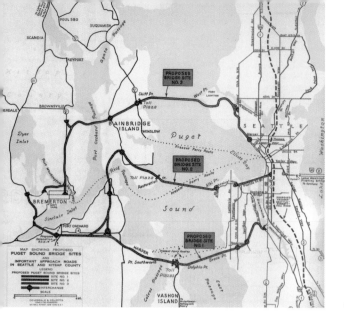

State plans in the 1950s called for replacing ferries with cross-sound bridges and tunnels.

from that disaster. They used perforated girders and open deck grating to allow wind to pass through and a wider roadway less prone to twisting. From then on aerodynamic testing was standard procedure in designing suspension bridges.

Also in October 1950, the department opened a new bridge over the Columbia between Wenatchee and East Wenatchee. Designed by highway department engineer George Stevens, the span was judged the most beautiful bridge of its type by the American Institute of Steel Construction in 1951. It was recently renamed in honor of State Senator George Sellars.

State Highway Commission

Led by Julia Butler Hansen, a veteran Democratic state representative from Cathlamet, Wahkiakum County, and chair of the House Roads and Bridges Committee, the 1951 Legislature passed sweeping administrative changes and substantial funding increases for the highway department. Throughout her tenure in the Legislature (1939–1960) and then the U.S. House of Representatives (1960–1974), Hansen was a formidable and effective advocate for highways and road building. She was the driving force behind the 1951 bill creating a five-member Highway Commission to run the department, which Governor Langlie signed even though it diminished his power over the department.

Since the 1929 abolition of the feuding Highway Committee, control had rested with the Highway Director, a political appointee of the governor, resulting in a new director and often a new direction whenever a new governor was elected. The creation of a bipartisan commission that would appoint the director and exercise ultimate authority was intended to insulate the department from political influences and ensure greater continuity. No more than three of the five members could be from the same political party; in addition, no more than three could be from the same side of the Cascades, and each had to be from a different Congressional district. Governor Langlie,

Legislature reorganizes the Department of Highways under a new five-member Highway Commission (which retains William Bugge as director), raises maximum speed limit to 60 m.p.h., expands authorization for limited-access highways, and authorizes $66.7 million in highway construction bonds in March 1951.

Washington State Toll Bridge Authority takes over Black Ball Line, at a cost of $6.8 million, on June 1, 1951.

New Northport Bridge opens over the Columbia River on June 13, 1951.

First meeting of Highway Commission elects Fred Redmon chair on July 9, 1951.

although not eager to relinquish his direct control over the highway department, was able to put his stamp on the commission as he appointed the first set of commissioners to staggered terms (subsequent terms were for six years).

The first members of the Highway Commission were Fred G. Redmon, L. B. Wallace, Ray A. Moisio, John E. Maley, and George B. Simpson. Redmon, a Yakima County commissioner, was elected chairman at the commission's first meeting in July 1951. At the same meeting, the commission retained Langlie appointee William Bugge as Director of Highways. Bugge ended up serving a total of 14 years (1949–1963), longer than any other highway department head.

Representative Hansen also guided passage of bonds for nearly $67 million, by far the biggest issue in the department's history to that point, to substantially boost the highway building program. It was the first in a steady stream of increases, soon joined by increased federal funding, as road construction accelerated through most of the decade. The bulk of the bond money went to Highway 99; the rest went to projects that included "four-laning" the Snoqualmie Pass highway, building the Pasco-Kennewick Bridge, retiring bonds for the Agate Pass Toll Bridge, and road building in the Columbia Basin.

Additional 1951 legislation included a more effective limited-access highway law and an increase in the maximum speed limit to 60 miles per hour. The 1951 law allowed the department to close connections to existing roads (upon paying adjoining owners compensation for the loss of access), making it feasible to upgrade those roads to take advantage of the new speed limit. Indeed, a department survey showed that not one existing road on the west side of the state was currently safe at 60 miles per hour. The Mercer Island section of U.S. Highway 10 (the forerunner of I-90), where frontage roads had controlled access from the time the section opened along with the floating bridge in 1940, became an official limited-access highway in 1952 after grade separations were made at key intersections under authority of the 1951 law.

The first State Highway Commission, chaired by Fred Redmon, center, in 1952.

62

Snow sheds eased winter driving over Snoqualmie Pass in the early 1950s. Below: 200 idling vehicles test Battery Street Tunnel ventilation, 1954.

In June 1951, the department opened a new bridge across the Columbia at Northport, Stevens County, the northernmost of the state's Columbia River crossings. It replaced a deteriorated timber structure originally built in 1897 as a railroad bridge. Later that summer, the road over White Pass southeast of Mt. Rainier was dedicated. White Pass was kept open all year (unlike nearby Chinook Pass which had opened 20 years earlier but is still today closed in the winter) and provided another route across the mountains, helping to relieve traffic over Snoqualmie Pass.

Ambitious Plans

As agreed in 1949, Alexander Peabody's Puget Sound Navigation Company transferred the bulk of its Black Ball Line ferry system to the state on June 1, 1951. The transition went smoothly, with little immediate change other than the process of repainting Black Ball's red and black smokestacks in the green trim that became a signature of the new Washington State Ferries (WSF). Most Black Ball employees stayed on with WSF, which was run by the Toll Bridge Authority under the Director of Highways. Floyd McDowell, the first general manager of WSF, took over Captain Peabody's office at Colman Dock on the Seattle waterfront.

Across Alaskan Way from the ferry headquarters, construction was progressing on the highway department's massive project to reroute traffic on Highway 99 (still

the state's primary north-south highway) around downtown Seattle on a waterfront viaduct. The concept dated from the late 1930s, when it was proposed by Seattle traffic engineer J. W. A. Bollong and local newspapers published futuristic renderings of the elevated expressway. The Depression and then World War II delayed implementation of the plan, but the highway department eventually began work on the Alaskan Way Viaduct in 1948. The first section of the Viaduct opened in 1953 (a southern extension came later). The next year saw the opening of the Battery Street tunnel carrying Highway 99 under the north end of downtown Seattle to the viaduct.

Even before the Highway 99 viaduct and tunnel were completed, plans were being made for an entirely new highway through Seattle from Everett to Tacoma, a road that would ultimately become Interstate 5. The state initially envisioned the new limited-access route as a tollway. Governor Langlie, who had been elected to an unprecedented third (but nonconsecutive) term in the 1952 election that saw Dwight Eisenhower win the White House and Henry Jackson join Warren Magnuson in the Senate, argued that counting on regular gas-tax revenue to pay for the project was unrealistic. Seattle officials objected to the toll concept and studies suggested it would be difficult for tolls to cover the projected costs.

MADAM CHAIRWOMAN

Julia Butler Hansen, born in 1907, was Washington state's most successful female Democratic politician of her era. She began her 43-year political career in 1937 when she was asked to run for city council in her hometown of Cathlamet and became its first woman member. Always advancing at the request of others, she became the first woman in the state to head a county Democratic committee. Elected to Congress in 1960, she was also the first to head a Congressional appropriations subcommittee.

Hansen won a State House seat in 1938. She joined the House Committee for Roads and Bridges in 1947. She missed being the first female Speaker of the State House by one vote in 1954, but was subsequently named Speaker of the House Pro Tempore. She was largely responsible for establishing the Highway Commission in 1951 and chaired the House Highway Committee for 11 years. Dubbed William Bugge's "legislative twin," Hansen helped to plan the network of roads and highways that shaped Washington's future development. She also was prominent in the establishment of a highway department merit system and a financial structure to pay for the highway system. She planned to retire in 1960, but when Congressman Russell Mack died in office that year, she won election to represent the 3rd Congressional District in southwest Washington.

Hansen retired from Congress in 1974 and headed home to Cathlamet. In January 1975, Governor Dan Evans appointed her to the State Highway Commission and the Washington State Toll Bridge Authority. After creation of the Transportation Commission in 1977, she served as its second chair from 1979–1980. She stepped down in 1980, moved back home to Calthlamet, and died in 1988. "I was simply taught that it was my duty to serve," she said of her career.

Building Seattle's Alaskan Way Viaduct, ca. 1953.

Ultimately the state Supreme Court ruled out toll funding, but by then federal interstate highway funds had become available.

State and local officials differed on other aspects of the new highway through central Seattle. The City's Transit Commission urged the highway department to include a 50-foot median that could accommodate a rail transit right of way but the state was only willing to consider express bus service. This accommodation would evolve into I-5's reversible express lanes but frustrate future transit planners.

The route that would become I-5 was just one part of a vast network of highways to, through, and around Seattle that 1950s highway engineers were proposing. A push was on for a second floating bridge across Lake Washington, although disputes over where to locate the bridge would delay the project for some years. Other contemplated routes, such as Seattle's "ring road" system, never came to fruition.

Department planners on the opposite side of Washington began drafting designs to expand U.S. 10 (now I-90) in the early 1950s. They sought to rise above Spokane's tangle of intersections and railroad crossings, but their proposed route angered local residents. The department pushed forward and completed the East Central section of the expanded U.S. 10 in 1958.

When Washington State Ferries began operations, many thought it was just a matter of time before ferries were replaced by a series of bridges spanning Puget Sound. Preliminary plans were drawn up for bridges from Seattle to Bainbridge and Vashon islands and connections from Bainbridge across Rich Passage and from Vashon to Southworth. However, the high cost of bridging the deep salt water of the sound and squabbles among supporters of different bridge routes kept plans on the drawing board. By the end of the decade many islanders no longer wanted cross-sound bridges.

Even while bridges were still considered a viable option, WSF

"Blue Bridge" opens between Pasco and Kennewick on July 30, 1954.

Department of Highways begins using its first "computer," an IBM Cardatype, in March 1956.

President Dwight D. Eisenhower signs new Federal Aid Highway Act, which boosts federal match to 90 percent to create an "Interstate and Defense Highway System" on June 29, 1956.

The Steamboat Slough and Snohomish River bridges in Everett, Skagit River Bridge in Mt. Vernon, Chehalis River Bridge in Aberdeen, and Wenatchee River Bridge all open between 1954 and 1956.

The ferry Rhododendron *and the Dash-80 prototype of the Boeing 707 (below) both "arrived" in 1954.*

began adding to the fleet it acquired in 1951. The first additions were two ferries purchased from Maryland that entered service on Puget Sound in 1954 as the *Rhododendron* and *Olympic*. Later that year the *Evergreen State,* the first ferry built for WSF, was launched. Many noted that the state was not following the long-standing Puget Sound tradition of giving ferries Indian names, and the Toll Bridge Authority acceded to public demand. The next two Evergreen State class ferries were named *Klahowya* and *Tillikum* — Chinook jargon words for "greetings" and "friends" or "people." WSF continued to give Indian names to subsequent vessels.

65

Jets and Interstates

Though water transportation would continue to play a significant role in Washington into the twenty-first century, dramatic new developments were occurring in the state's skies. On July 15, 1954, the Dash-80 prototype of the Boeing 707 jet airliner made its maiden flight from Boeing Field and when it entered service four years later became the first really successful commercial jet airliner.

With the success of the 707, officials at Sea-Tac realized that the airport would need to expand to accommodate the advent of jet travel. The main runway had already been extended to 7,500 feet in 1950 but it and the terminal would have to grow again by the time regular jet service began in 1959.

As dramatic as the rise of jet passenger travel was, the most far-reaching transportation development of the decade, whose effects transformed the state and nation, was passage of the Federal Aid Highway Act of 1956 providing for a federally funded nationwide system of "Interstate and Defense Highways." The federal government had aided states with road construction funds since 1916, but until 1956 the states still shouldered the bulk of the costs. By the 1950s it was apparent not only in Washington state but across the country that local funding sources could not meet the rising demand for new roads stemming from a decade of postwar prosperity. Roads were jammed, traffic deaths skyrocketed, and newspapers talked of a highway crisis.

Timeline

King County voters reject first proposal for Municipality of Metropolitan Seattle (including transportation authority) in March 1958. A narrower Metro limited to water quality is adopted in September.

Olympia Freeway Bypass (portion of future I-5) opens on December 12, 1958.

The south extension of Seattle's Alaskan Way Viaduct opens to traffic on September 3, 1959.

Vancouver-Portland Interstate Toll Bridge over the Columbia River opens in January 1960.

Putting aside his usual reservations about federal interference in state affairs, Governor Langlie joined officials from other states to lobby Congress and the Eisenhower administration for an infusion of federal funds as the only solution to the crisis. President Eisenhower, like his fellow Republican Langlie, generally opposed federal public works projects. But the president believed that more cars and more highways brought national happiness. He endorsed what was described as the biggest, most expensive public works project in world history.

The initial plan called for construction over the next 20 years of 41,000 miles of limited-access freeways across the country, connecting virtually all cities with more than 50,000 people. The new interstates were unlike existing roads — there would be no stoplights or stop signs, grade crossings or roadside development. The federal government would pay 90 percent of the cost, in part by raising the federal gas tax from two to four cents per gallon.

Washington was allocated an estimated $750 million to construct approximately 740 miles of the 41,000-mile national system (local and national figures would grow over time with the addition of "pet projects"). Although officials from around the state sought federal interstate funds for their own pet projects, the state's top priority was construction of the long-desired Seattle freeway from Everett to Tacoma as part of the planned Interstate 5, followed closely by improving U.S. Highway 10 in Spokane and over Snoqualmie Pass to four-lane limited-access standards and replacing the Columbia River bridges at Vancouver and Vantage.

Emphasizing the pre-eminence of I-5 in the state's highway planning, the highway department made the first major change in the six-district organization since Webster Hoover was Highway Engineer, forming a seventh district whose sole responsibility was construction of the interstate through Seattle. (District 7 was later given charge of portions of I-90 and I-405 as well.)

As highway construction increased in volume and complexity, highway engineers began turning to computers to speed calculations previously performed by hand. The department's Plans and Contracts Division acquired an IBM "Cardatype Unit" early in

Building the Pasco-Kennewick Blue Bridge in 1954.

1956. By that fall, the department formed a Computer Section and made 44 computer applications available. The increased pace of construction prompted the department to step up recruitment of civil engineering graduates, whose numbers were temporarily declining even as demand rose.

There was always plenty of work for bridge engineers. The second highway bridge between Pasco and Kennewick over the Columbia, an unnamed span called the "Blue Bridge" because of its

Olympia Bypass (future I-5), ca. 1958.

unique color, opened in 1954 and was followed in the next two years by the Snohomish River and Steamboat Slough bridges between Everett and Marysville, the Skagit River Bridge in Mt. Vernon, the Wenatchee River Bridge, and the Chehalis River Bridge in Aberdeen.

In the 1956 election, Democrat Albert D. Rosellini succeeded Governor Langlie, who made an unsuccessful attempt to gain Magnuson's senate seat, while Eisenhower was easily re-elected president. As governor, Rosellini made highway construction a top priority. He resolved the long-running debate over where to locate a second floating bridge across Lake Washington by successfully pushing the Evergreen Point to Union Bay crossing. (Years later the Evergreen Point bridge was officially renamed in honor of Rosellini.)

By the end of Rosellini's first term, construction had started on the Evergreen Point Bridge and was well underway on another floating bridge, across the challenging mouth of Hood Canal to cut driving time to the Olympic Peninsula. Development of both bridges was directed by senior bridge engineer Charles Andrew, who had earlier overseen construction of the first Lake Washington Floating Bridge and both Tacoma Narrows bridges.

Looking to the Future

By the late 1950s, the long-discussed highway across the North Cascades looked like it might soon become a reality. Boosters on both sides of the mountains formed the North Cross-State Highway Association in 1953 and worked hard lobbying department officials and state legislators, including a skeptical Julia Butler Hansen. They also found success with the federal government, persuading the Bureau of Public Roads and the Forest Service to approve timber access roads and build them to state standards for eventual inclusion in the state highway system.

In 1957, District 2 Engineer Ike Munson, who had surveyed the highway route a quarter century earlier, made another trip across the mountains, this time guiding

Tacoma Freeway (future I-5), ca. 1960.

highway commissioners and others along the proposed highway. Munson was joined by George Zahn, a Methow orchardist who became one of the leading promoters of the North Cross-State Highway (as it was then called) and later a highway commissioner. Despite their efforts it was another 15 years before the North Cascades Highway actually opened.

Federal approval and funding for the first portion of I-5 through Seattle came in October 1957. By then, early indications of what would later become an all-out anti-freeway movement were already being heard. Architects and engineers joined downtown business owners in arguing that a deep open ditch through downtown Seattle was not the best location for the interstate. However, plans for that route had been underway for much of the decade and most political and civic leaders opposed the delay that would result from finding an alternative.

An innovative proposal for a lid covering the freeway to mitigate the damage was considered, but also rejected because of the delay it would involve. (The concept was successfully revived decades later for Freeway Park over I-5 and for several I-90 lids). By 1958, the state began condemnation of the homes, businesses, and other property in the path of the freeway — 4,500 parcels were taken in Seattle alone and a total of 6,600 parcels between Tacoma and Everett.

Some tentative steps toward region-wide transportation planning were taken by the end of the decade. As early as 1953, the state chapter of the American Institute of Architects urged coordination of the substantial and mostly unplanned post-war growth in the Puget Sound area. After three years of informal consultation, local governments in King, Kitsap, Pierce, and Snohomish counties formed the Puget Sound Regional Planning Conference, soon renamed Puget Sound Governmental Council (PSGC). In 1960, the Highway Department teamed with PSGC, the federal Bureau of Public Roads, and other state and federal agencies to launch the $1.6 million Puget Sound Regional Transportation Study. The study, which lasted six years, was one of the first large scale efforts at comprehensive planning for transportation and land use.

Voters pass Referendum 207, replacing merit system with civil service for highway employees, on November 8, 1960.

Washington's population exceeds 2,853,000 and the Highway Commission lists more than 6,500 miles of improved state highways in 1960.

Another regional transportation concept was temporarily sidetracked in March 1958 when King County voters turned down plans for a Municipality of Metropolitan Seattle to run a variety of regional services including a transit system. Several months later voters approved a pared back "Metro" that dealt only with water quality, especially cleaning up the seriously polluted Lake Washington. It was 1972 before Metro gained transportation authority.

In 1959, the first contracts were awarded for constructing Interstate 82 between Ellensburg and Union Gap just south of Yakima. The Yakima and Naches River bridges and Selah Interchange were finished in 1960, but it took 14 years to complete this first section and a total of 30 years to build all of I-82. The Vancouver-Portland Interstate Toll Bridge opened to traffic in 1960. The project involved rebuilding the original 1917 bridge and building a matching span to the west. The twin bridges provided an important link in the development of I-5, carrying the freeway across the Columbia River.

Voters in the 1960 election approved Initiative 207 creating a civil service system for state employees. In addition to a State Personnel Board covering most departments, the initiative created a separate Highway Department Personnel Board, appointed by the commission, in place of the merit system that previously covered highway department employees. Governor Rosellini was re-elected and John F. Kennedy narrowly won the presidency.

As the young president took office, Washingtonians looked hopefully to the future. The modern interstate highway system was becoming a reality, jets were filling the skies, and futurists prepared to showcase yet more innovations in transportation and other technology at the upcoming Century 21 World's Fair. Few envisioned the turmoil and tragedies that also lay ahead, the sweeping and at times divisive transformation in social, cultural, and political attitudes that would impact transportation along with the rest of society.

Governor Albert Rosellini opens Tacoma Freeway, 1960.

Seattle Freeway (now I-5) construction, ca. 1961. Below: Ford "Seattle-ite" concept car, 1962.

1961~1977: Pedal to the Metal

Despite a slight decline in federal interstate funds due to a national recession, the 1960s began with bright promise for the Department of Highways. A young, energetic President Kennedy unveiled a "New Frontier" for the nation and set his sights on nothing less than the Moon, and the entire state focused on the 1962 World's Fair in Seattle. Its Space Needle, Monorail, and a six-wheeled, nuclear-powered Ford concept car called the Seattle-ite XXI symbolized the technology-driven prosperity and comfort that awaited Washingtonians in "Century 21."

Closer to the here and now, the Legislature raised the gas tax to 7.5 cents to maintain progress on Interstate 5 and numerous other projects. With the support of Governor Albert D. Rosellini and citizen groups such as Allied Arts and the Evergreen Safety Council, Washington enacted

a sweeping Highway Advertising Control Act in March 1961 to ban and remove billboards visible from interstate roadways — four years before Lady Bird Johnson promoted the National Highway Beautification Act of 1965. The latter act would make federal funds available for rest areas on interstates, a field in which Washington would become a design leader.

But other forces were also gathering strength. On June 5, 1961, some 100 Seattle residents and community activists staged a "walk the ditch" protest against Interstate 5. They objected to the highway trench that would sever First Hill from the downtown, and leading architects such as Victor Steinbrueck and Paul Thiry proposed a "lid" over I-5 to reconnect the communities.

The Highway Commission rejected the idea as impractical and too expensive, although unstable soil and landslides along the route would later make engineers wish they had chosen a different route. Ironically, many years later much of the downtown freeway would be lidded over by Freeway Park and the State Convention & Trade Center.

It was easy to overlook warning signs of the political turmoil to come as the Hood Canal Floating Bridge opened on August 12, 1961, and work was completed on the soaring Interstate 5 bridge over the Lake Washington Ship Canal, then the largest steel truss bridge in the Pacific Northwest. Construction also advanced on the Evergreen Point (now Albert D. Rosellini) Floating Bridge across Lake Washington.

As the World's Fair opened in April 1962, Metro hoped that excitement over the new Alweg Monorail would encourage King County voters to activate its latent regional transportation planning authority. The AAA opposed the measure, claiming that Metro was secretly planning a "wheel tax" on cars and trucks. They won this first of many skirmishes to come between transit and highway interests, and vague ideas to extend the monorail to Sea-Tac Airport went nowhere. For the near term, highways remained the pathways to the future.

Hood Canal Floating Bridge opens for a nuclear submarine. Above: Seattle's Monorail and Space Needle, 1962.

New Vantage Bridge, ca. 1970. Below: Evergreen Point Floating Bridge charged tolls until 1979.

Ramping Up

In his final biennial report to the Legislature, Highway Director William Bugge detailed $146 million in construction projects — up by more than half from 1958–1960 — around the state. A major milestone in 1962 was completion of a new Vantage Bridge over the Columbia. In an example of massive recycling, the old Vantage Bridge was disassembled, stored, and later reassembled at Lyons Ferry, where it entered service in 1968.

New or replacement bridges also opened across the Cowlitz River at Longview and over the Chehalis River at Montesano. After

12 years of construction, SR 105 was finally finished along the north shore of Willapa Bay, cutting the driving distance between Tokeland and South Bend from 70 miles to just 23.

East of the Cascades, the Biggs Rapids Bridge opened over the Columbia between Maryhill and Biggs, Oregon. (It was rededicated as the Sam Hill Memorial Bridge in 1964 to honor the Good Roads activist.) Work also began on Interstate 82 to replace the treacherous Canyon Road between Ellensburg and Yakima, but battles over its ultimate path to the Columbia would rage into the 1980s.

Things were not going so smoothly in the Washington State Ferries system. The Highway Commission discharged its director and gave the helm to veteran Navy engineer Charles G. Prahl in September 1962. That same year, Congress mandated "continuous transportation planning" for metropolitan areas, launching major regional studies for Puget Sound, Vancouver-Portland, Spokane, and Lewiston-Clarkston, and spurring creation of intergovernmental organizations on the model of the Puget Sound Governmental Conference.

In March 1963, the Legislature established a scheme to prioritize highway projects on the basis of the size of communities they served. It also ended six decades of fiddling with highway numbers by establishing the present system of uniform SR ("Sign Route," now "State Route") designations.

PRAHL AT THE HELM

Charles G. Prahl joined the highway department as manager of Washington State Ferries after a 22-year Navy career. Born in 1913, Prahl grew up in Ontario, Oregon. After earning a civil engineering degree from Oregon State University in 1935, he worked on the Grand Coulee reclamation project in Eastern Washington.

Entering the Navy in 1940, Prahl received a Bronze Star for his service commanding a Seabee battalion on Okinawa in 1945. He worked on naval construction projects around the world, ultimately taking charge of all Navy construction in the Northwest.

Shortly after retiring from the Navy in 1962, Prahl was appointed to head the ferry system. A year later, the Highway Commission appointed him director. Prahl oversaw construction of major portions of Washington's interstate highway system, reorganized the department, and implemented innovative programs such as a highway classification system seen as a national model.

Prahl's tenure was a turbulent time for the department. Attitudes toward transportation were shifting. He clashed repeatedly with a growing movement that opposed some major freeway projects and demanded more support for mass transit. Facing mounting criticism, and amid reports of friction with Governor Dan Evans, Prahl resigned in 1969.

Prahl became a vice president of Seattle's General Construction Company, where he worked on the Alaska oil pipeline. He retired in 1975 and died in 1984.

Governor Dan Evans dedicates I-5 in Seattle, 1967.

On August 28, 1963, the long-awaited Evergreen Point Floating Bridge opened to traffic. Earlier that year, William Bugge resigned after guiding the department for 14 years. The Highway Commission did not have to look far for an able successor and tapped Washington State Ferries manager Charles Prahl on October 21.

The assassination of President John F. Kennedy a month later stunned and saddened the nation, but President Lyndon Johnson's vision of a "Great Society" also created new opportunities. The physical and social needs of America's cities were special concerns of Johnson's, and his good friend Senator Warren G. Magnuson pressed the case for expanded public transportation funding that led to passage of the Urban Mass Transportation Act of 1964. Johnson also strengthened the roles of "metropolitan planning organizations" in federal transportation funding, elevating the influence of local and regional governments to counterbalance state highway agencies.

Highways remained the state's chief concern, however, and they had no more ardent advocate than Prahl. In 1964, the department's official magazine, *Washington Highways*, boasted that new roadways had already cut the travel time between Vancouver and Blaine from 11 hours in 1935 to five, and from 11 hours to seven between Seattle and Spokane. It also noted that during the past 30 years, vehicle registrations had more than tripled from 515,000 to 1.7 million while the population had only doubled. "Thus the picture emerges," it commented: "More autos, more drivers, more going, and for more reasons ... and this causes the flood of vehicles, which creates the necessity for more and bigger highways."

By the end of 1964, Washington state had received more than $589 million in federal road funds since 1916, most of it since 1956 during the terms of Governor Rosellini. But his record as road builder and the "Johnson Landslide" over Senator Barry Goldwater were not enough to push Rosellini's bid for a third term over the finish line. He lost in November

President John F. Kennedy is assassinated in Dallas on November 22, 1963, and Lyndon B. Johnson takes office.

Biggs Rapids Bridge (completed in 1962) over the Columbia River is rededicated as the Sam Hill Memorial Bridge on June 19, 1964.

Congress passes the Urban Mass Transportation Act in 1964.

Department of Highways undergoes a major reorganization during 1965.

Interstate 5 opens to traffic between Seattle and Everett on February 3, 1965, and Seattle reversible lanes open in June.

Interstate 405 opens between Renton and Tukwila on September 3, 1965.

Congress passes National Highway Beautification Act on October 22, 1965.

New Seattle Ferry Terminal opens at Colman Dock on May 18, 1966.

Federal funds became available in 1965 for interstate rest areas. Below: New Colman Dock and state ferries were launched in 1966.

1964 to Daniel Evans, a young and liberal Republican State Senator and civil engineer from north Seattle who offered his own "Blueprint for Progress."

75

As Dan Evans settled into office, drivers began to take advantage of Interstate 5, reducing traffic on old Pacific Highway 99 by two thirds. The section of Interstate 5 between Everett and Seattle and the latter city's new express lanes opened in 1965, monitored by an innovative remote television and control system. Renton's I-405/SR 167 interchange was completed and the gap on SR 26 between Vantage and Washtucna was closed. At the same time, mounting traffic on the old Sunset Highway (the future I-90) required installation of what became a notorious stop light in North Bend.

Rising traffic volumes also impacted the ferry system, which was overdue for expansion and modernization. The department tried to arrange construction of four new "Super Ferries" with local shipyards, but could not reach agreement. In late 1965, the Highway Commission reluctantly authorized Prahl to award the $22.3 million contract to a San Diego firm. (First Lady Nancy Evans would christen the first vessel, the *Hyak*, one year later on December 17, 1966.)

On August 27, 1966, the Astoria Bridge opened across the mouth of the Columbia. The 4.1-mile span was built by the Oregon Highway Department at a cost of $24 million, with financial and technical aid from Washington State. A week later, the Highway

SEATTLE FERRY TERMINAL
MAY 18th, 1966 at 10:30 a.m.

WASHINGTON STATE HIGHWAY COMMISSION

Building I-5

Recognizing that U.S. 99 would soon be overwhelmed by growing traffic, especially where it passed through city centers, the highway department began planning an expanded north-south highway in the early 1950s. When passage of the 1956 Federal Aid Highway Act eliminated the need for tolls to finance construction through downtown Seattle and other cities, work began in earnest.

Construction of the new freeway's 277 centerline miles generally followed the route of old U.S. 99 and incorporated some newer four-lane stretches built in greater Vancouver and Olympia. Interstate 5's most daunting right-of-way passed through Seattle's dense neighborhoods — requiring purchase of some 4,500 parcels of land mostly occupied by homes and apartment buildings. It also entailed construction of a major bridge across the Lake Washington Ship Canal and squeezing a multi-lane highway between slide-prone hills and established financial and industrial areas. The latter challenge was partially addressed through the innovation of reversible "express lanes" to handle rush hour traffic between Seattle's Northgate area and its downtown.

The first segment of I-5 formally opened in Tacoma on December 21, 1960, and the freeway was completed incrementally through May 1969, when the last temporary stop light was removed north of Everett. A final cost is difficult to calculate, given that a freeway of the size and complexity of Interstate 5 is never really "finished," but the total construction bill (not counting right of way) was estimated at $235 million in 1970 — $1.2 billion in 2005 dollars.

Department and Puget Sound Governmental Council (PSGC, now Puget Sound Regional Council) released the results of a six-year regional transportation study, and set off a political storm.

Forward Thrust to Boeing Bust

The report predicted that the combined population of King, Pierce, Kitsap, and Snohomish counties would balloon to 2.75 million by 1990, and that most of this growth would occur outside of established cities. Such a dispersed populace could only be served by building more highways, planners reasoned, and they had plenty to propose, including a cross-sound bridge via Vashon Island, a third Lake Washington floating bridge between Sand Point and Kirkland, and a new "Eastside Freeway" between I-405 and Lake Sammamish.

Many residents in the path of these proposed improvements were alarmed, especially on Vashon Island. Mass transit advocates were also furious with the study's "faint praise" for the potential value of rapid rail systems, although they were not surprised. Anticipating the study's pro-highway conclusions, the PSGC had commissioned an independent analysis of rail transit by DeLeuw Cather. Its more optimistic findings were published in late 1965 and became the basis for the "Forward Thrust" rail plan of 1968.

Spokane Freeway (now I-90) in the 1960s. Below: A sign of the Boeing Bust.

By the end of 1966, annual state highway spending had topped $100 million for the second year in a row, and departmental staffing had grown to more than 4,000 employees. The last section of Interstate 5 between Everett and Tacoma was ready to open (the Vernita Bridge on the northern edge of the Hanford Reservation had opened the year before), and tolls were removed from the Tacoma Narrows, Fox Island, Longview, and Vancouver-Portland Interstate bridges.

Unfortunately, federal highway aid was on the chopping block as the bills came due for the Great Society and the war in Vietnam. The Legislature raised the gas tax to nine cents per gallon in 1967 to help fill the gap. It also expanded the Aeronautics Commission to seven seats, raised aviation fuel taxes by two cents to implement a new State Airport Aid program, and levied registration fees on private pilots to help fund aircraft safety, rescue, and education programs.

Growth in the Puget Sound region, especially on the Kitsap Peninsula and Bainbridge Island, combined with the aging of the ferry system's fleet — many vessels dated from the original Black Ball Line — demanded construction of new, faster, and bigger boats. Two new Super Ferries, the *Kaleetan* and *Elwha*, were launched in 1967, along with the smaller *Hiyu,* which replaced the aging *Skansonia.* The final member of the Super Ferry class, the *Yakima*, entered service in 1968, while the last cable ferry on the Snake River was retired with dedication of the new (actually recycled) Lyons Ferry Bridge.

More milestones were passed in 1968. In May, the U.S. 12 Cowlitz River Bridge opened

Oregon Highway Department opens Astoria Bridge over the Columbia River on August 27, 1966.

Puget Sound Regional Transportation Study recommends cross-sound bridges and opposes rail transit in September 1966.

First Super Ferry, *Hyak,* is launched in San Diego on December 17, 1966.

Final 17.2-mile section of I-5 between Everett and Tacoma opens on January 31, 1967.

U.S. Department of Transportation is established on April 1, 1967.

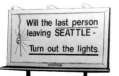

Will the last person leaving SEATTLE - Turn out the lights.

Recycled Vantage Bridge truss spans formed the Lyons Ferry Bridge in 1968.

WSF retires the ferry
Kalakala on August 6,
1967.

King County voters
reject "Forward Thrust"
bonds for regional
rail transit system on
February 13, 1968 (and
again in 1970).

Cowlitz River Bridge,
then North America's
longest concrete arch
bridge, opens on U.S. 12
in May 1968.

Boeing 747 "Jumbo Jet"
makes its maiden flight
from Everett's Paine
Field on February 9,
1969.

in Lewis County as North America's longest concrete arch span at
530 feet. On September 29, Governor Evans, Senator Magnuson, and
Congressman Lloyd Meeds turned out to celebrate the first vehicular
crossing of the SR 20 North Cascades Highway route (the highway itself
was still four years from completion). The last permanent stop light on
the I-5 corridor was removed in November 1968, as construction was
completed between Lacey and Fort Lewis.

As 1969 began, the end of the long road to build Interstate 5 was
in sight, and it should have marked a professional triumph for Highway
Director Charles Prahl, but he would depart in May amid an increasingly
bitter debate over the future of the state transportation system. The
seeds of the conflict were sown in King County. Urban visionaries led by
Metro co-founder James Ellis organized a regional coalition to win bond
funding for new parks, roads, sewers, and a "domed stadium" to revital-
ize the city core and cope with suburban sprawl. The centerpiece of the
plan was a rapid rail transit system modeled on San Francisco's BART.

Thanks to Washington's powerful congressional delegation, the federal government was ready to cover most of the system's $1.155 billion cost, but a 60 percent majority of voters needed to approve bonds for the $385 million match.

The rail plan pitted highway interests and suburban developers against Seattle-based neighborhood activists and progressives — including Governor Evans and most of the city's state legislators. The debate was heated by mounting local opposition to expansion of Interstate 90 and a new R. H. Thomson Expressway, and framed philosophically by both sides as "either" transit "or" highways, although the plan would have little or no impact on state road funds. On February 13, 1968, a slim majority of skeptical voters approved the plan, but not enough to authorize the bonds.

Undaunted, transit boosters increased pressure in Olympia for state assistance for mass transit, which in turn alarmed representatives of smaller cities and rural communities, especially east of the Cascades, as well as highway supporters. With Governor Evans's support, the urban coalition won approval of a 1 percent motor vehicle excise tax (MVET) to match local transit funds.

The actual money involved was small, but the legislation sidestepped Amendment 18 to the State Constitution and breached the high walls surrounding state road funds. Passage of the transit motor vehicle excise tax was also the first step in Evans's drive to transform the Highway Department and Commission into a multi-modal transportation agency answering to the governor. Charles Prahl and many on the existing commission did not agree, and they did not mince words.

In his January 1969 biennial report, Prahl conceded, "there appears to be considerable resistance to the construction of new highways, particularly in urban areas," and acknowledged "the need for other modes of transportation." However, he warned against "threats to Motor Vehicle Funds" from "proposals to divert these funds to other purposes" — especially rapid transit. He argued that "such facilities should be provided for from additional tax monies if they, in fact, have any merit."

The last stop light on Interstate 5 from Blaine to Vancouver is removed in May 1969.

Governor Evans signs legislation permitting local governments to levy a 1 percent motor vehicle excise tax (MVET) for transit services on May 23, 1969.

Cowlitz River Bridge featured America's longest concrete arch in 1968.

George H. Andrews becomes acting Director of Highways after Prahl resigns in May 1969, and is appointed director on August 19, 1969.

Spokane's 4th Avenue viaduct is completed in September 1969.

80

Department of Highways occupies its new headquarters (the current Transportation Building) in Olympia in 1970.

Astoria Bridge (Mark Bozanich)

When Governor Evans signed the transit MVET bill on May 23, 1969, Charles Prahl had already tendered his resignation. That same month, the last temporary stop light was removed from Interstate 5 in Everett. Although substantial work remained around Olympia, Chehalis, and Vancouver, one could finally drive I-5 nonstop from the Columbia River to British Columbia. On the opposite side of the state, Spokane's 4th Avenue viaduct opened, completing its downtown freeway.

The Highway Commission named Prahl's deputy, George Andrews, to take his place. Unlike his predecessor, Andrews avowed "that public transport was key to solving future transportation problems," but others still needed convincing. The Forward Thrust rapid transit plan failed to garner even a simple majority when it was submitted anew to King County voters in March 1970. Many blamed the deepening "Boeing Bust" aerospace recession, which would stall the entire state over the next five years. Meanwhile, a billion dollars of federal funds reserved for Metro was re-allocated to build Atlanta's MARTA rail system.

Green Lights, Red Flags

On April 22, 1970, the nation observed the first Earth Day as the new Department of Highways headquarters in Olympia neared completion. Its Spartan, fortress-like façade bore witness to the social and political

SR 14 near Bingen, ca. 1970.

A BRIDGE BUILDER

In a nearly 35-year highway career, George Andrews worked his way through the ranks to the department's top position. Born in Kennewick in 1920, he joined the department in 1941 after graduating from Washington State University.

In the 28 years before he became Director of Highways in 1969, Andrews worked on paving projects, as a bridge engineer and construction engineer, and as district engineer for District 7, which handled construction of the Seattle Freeway (I-5). In 1965 he was named assistant director for highway development and in 1968 he became deputy director to Charles Prahl.

Andrews succeeded Prahl in 1969, in time to become the first tenant of the new Transportaton Building (right) in Olympia. Andrews served until 1975, guiding the department through a time of transition as it broadened its focus beyond highway construction to begin placing greater emphasis on mass transit and other transportation modes.

In 1973, after the American Association of State Highway Officials changed its name to American Association of State Highway and Transportation Officials, Andrews became the first president of the newly named transportation organization. He supported creation of a state transportation department to combine responsibility for roads, transit, railroads, and other modes.

He retired in 1975 and became vice president of transportation for the St. Louis-based Sverdrup Corporation, where he worked until 1982. George Andrews died at his Olympia home in 1988.

turmoil of the 1960s, which was reaching full boil. The department would undergo its own revolution over the next seven years.

The critical spark was struck by a seemingly innocuous requirement in the new National Environmental Policy Act (NEPA), crafted largely by Senator Henry M. Jackson and signed into law on January 1, 1970, by President Richard M. Nixon. The act mandated that nearly every new federal project — and projects receiving federal funds, such as highways — should prepare an "environmental impact statement," or EIS, assessing its potential effects on nature and communities and ways, including alternatives, to "mitigate" any harm prior to implementation. (A year later, the Legislature adopted a nearly identical requirement for state projects.)

First "Earth Day" is observed on April 22, 1970.

Seven Seattle residents file suit in federal court to compel preparation of an "environmental impact statement" (EIS) for planned expansion of Interstate 90 on May 28, 1970.

Seattle Transit inaugurates the state's first Park and Ride lot for new Blue Streak express bus service on September 8, 1970.

The first Jumbo Ferry was named for the Spokane Tribe.

Barely six months after NEPA was signed, Seattle residents led by Margaret Tunks and Roger Leeds sued to halt construction of I-90 through the city's Mount Baker neighborhood until an EIS was prepared. The federal courts agreed the following year, and a second lawsuit stopped work west of Snoqualmie Pass in 1972. Department planners scrambled to prepare their first EIS analyses, but they could not pass legal or technical muster. Construction of the last few miles of the Boston-to-Seattle freeway would not resume until 1979.

Puget Sound's transportation woes were compounded by the impending collapse of its existing public transit systems. City-owned Seattle Transit was running on fumes, despite the introduction of innovative "Blue Streak" express service and the state's first "Park and Ride" lot near the Northgate Shopping Center. Private suburban bus lines faced imminent bankruptcy.

Metro launched an intensive citizen participation effort to plan a regional all-bus system (without expensive and controversial light rail) and it returned to Olympia to win authority for a special three tenths of a percent sales tax to fund it, with local voter approval. It also secured new commitments for use of highway funds for park and ride lots and "high occupancy vehicle" (HOV) lanes, thereby allowing the State to aid transit-related improvements with gas-tax and MVET revenues without violating the 18th Amendment to the State Constitution. The Legislature would later attempt to renege, but the State Supreme Court held for Metro, and WSDOT became a major force in the development of park and ride lots and other transit-friendly highway improvements around the state.

East of the Cascades, highway projects were not immediately affected by the new environmental standards or by public opposition. Interstate 82's elegant Fred Redmon Memorial Bridge over Selah Creek was dedicated on November 2, 1971. Named for the first chair of the

Lorna Ream, the first woman to serve on the Highway Commission.

Congress rejects funding for Boeing-designed Supersonic Transport, triggering the regional "Boeing Bust" recession, on December 3, 1970.

Washington's population tops 3,413,000, and state highways and roads total 6,861 miles in 1970.

Amtrak, national passenger rail service, begins operation on May 1, 1971.

Fred Redmon Memorial Bridge opens on I-82 over Selah Creek on November 2, 1971.

Jumbo Ferries *Spokane* and *Walla Walla* are launched during 1972.

Seattle voters scrap the proposed Bay Freeway and revoke bonds previously issued for the R. H. Thomson Expressway on February 8, 1972.

North Cascades Highway (SR 20) opens between Newhalem and Winthrop on September 2, 1972.

Highway Commission, the 550-foot twin concrete arches claimed the record previously set by the Cowlitz River Bridge as the longest such span in North America. It was a short reprieve: Two years later environmental lawsuits halted work on the I-182 spur to the Tri-Cities.

The Highway Commission welcomed its first woman member, Lorna Ream from Spokane, in 1971. A longtime environmentalist and member of the 1965 Spokane Metropolitan Area Transportation Study committee, Ream was tapped by Governor Evans to fill the unexpired term of George Zahn, who had died in office, and to bring a broader perspective to the commission. "It was an enormous surprise," she said in a recent interview. "Dan wanted someone who looked at the total transportation system, not just at state roads." She encountered no problems as the commission's first female member: "I had a lot of experience working with men." By 1976, when she was reappointed to fill another partial term, women would constitute a majority of the Highway Commission.

On the last day of 1971, the Highway Commission joined with the Aeronautics Commission, Highway Patrol, Department of Motor Vehicles, Toll Bridge Authority, Traffic Safety Commission, and Urban Arterial Board to issue a combined Annual Report. It was a preview of the kind of comprehensive information a combined transportation

King County voters approve creation of Metro Transit on September 19, 1972.

State voters reject "Washington Futures" transportation bonds on November 7, 1972.

Aeronautics Commission adopts the first Washington State Airport System Plan on June 22, 1973.

America's longest concrete arch bridge when built in 1971, the Fred Redmon Bridge spans Selah Creek.

The new Metro Transit slapped stickers on Seattle buses and trolleys to launch service on January 1, 1973.

State's first acoustical freeway barriers and first High Occupancy Vehicle (HOV) lanes are introduced in 1973.

Spokane "Expo 74" World's Fair opens on May 4, 1974.

OPEC oil embargo spurs Congress to pass National Mass Transportation Act, providing the first federal aid for transit operating costs, and imposing a 55 m.p.h. freeway speed limit in 1974.

authority might produce, but the financial news was not good as hyper-inflation eroded the state's buying power and as major projects faced mounting public and legal challenges. Among the few bright spots, traffic fatalities were declining thanks to newer and safer roadways, and construction had begun on the new "Jumbo Ferries," *Spokane* and *Walla Walla*.

In February 1972, Seattle voters scrapped that city's plans for a "Bay Freeway" from I-5 to 99 and the R. H. Thomson Expressway through the Central Area. Although they preserved neighborhoods, the decisions would compound congestion on I-5 and SR 520 in future decades by eliminating planned highway capacity.

On September 2, 1972, Governor Evans presided at the official opening of the North Cascades Highway (SR 20) between Newhalem and Winthrop, fulfilling a promised "state road" first approved in 1893. The new highway was the last link in the "Cascade Loop" via SR 20, SR 153 from Winthrop to Wenatchee, SR 2 between Wenatchee and Puget Sound, the Mukilteo Ferry, and SR 525 back to SR 20 — acclaimed by *National Geographic Traveler* as "one of America's grandest, most spectacular drives."

Two weeks later, King County voters approved the new Metro Transit plan, finally putting the agency in the driver's seat on its fifth try since 1958. The rest of state balked, however, at funding $50 million in transit bonds as part of a "Washington Futures" package on the November 1972 ballot.

Work on the western terminus of I-90 remained stalled through 1973, but the Highway Department made progress on other fronts. It welcomed its second woman commissioner, Seattle activist Virginia Gunby; completed its first HOV lane, on SR 520 between Redmond and the Evergreen Point Floating Bridge; and erected the

Spokane's EXPO 74 World's Fair drew millions of visitors despite the OPEC oil embargo.

This 1954 Highway News *cartoon saw the road ahead.*

Regional Transportation Planning

When local officials from King, Kitsap, Pierce, and Snohomish counties formally organized the Puget Sound Governmental Conference (PSGC) in 1957 to coordinate regional planning, they did so on their own initiative. It was not until the Federal Aid Highway Act of 1962 that ongoing transportation planning on a regional basis — to include cities, suburbs, and outlying areas — was mandated by law. All metropolitan communities eligible for federal highway funds (those with a central city population of more than 50,000) were required to engage in continuous transportation planning as of July 1, 1965. Regional "conferences" and councils made up of elected officials undertook these tasks with the aid of professional staff, and they became forums for prioritizing transportation needs and reconciling urban, suburban, and rural viewpoints on growth management.

Puget Sound was well ahead of the curve because the Highway Commission, PSGC, and other state and federal agencies had launched the Puget Sound Regional Transportation Study in 1960. By the mid-1960s, transportation studies were also underway in the Vancouver-Portland, Spokane, Lewiston-Clarkston, Wenatchee, and Tri-Cities areas (some of which chose to undertake studies even though they were not required to do so).

The roles and authority of regional planning groups over transportation and other federally funded projects and programs expanded under the Intergovernmental Cooperation Act of 1968 and President Nixon's "New Federalism" reforms in the early 1970s. Greater power also raised the potential for intra-regional conflict. After its member jurisdictions clashed over regional planning goals and priorities, the PSGC reorganized as the Puget Sound Council of Governments (PSCOG) in 1977, and again as the Puget Sound Regional Council (PSRC) in 1990.

The requirement for ongoing planning was incorporated into the landmark Intermodal Surface Transportation Efficiency Act (ISTEA) of 1991, which calls for a Metropolitan Planning Organization (MPO) composed of elected officials in each urbanized area with a population over 50,000. MPOs cooperate with the State in ongoing planning for multiple modes of transportation.

As of early 2005, there were 11 MPOs in Washington: Benton Franklin Council of Governments, Cowlitz-Wahkiakum Council of Governments, Lewis Clark Valley Metropolitan Planning Organization, Puget Sound Regional Council, Skagit Council of Governments, Southwest Washington Regional Transportation Council, Spokane Regional Transportation Council, Thurston Regional Planning Council, Wenatchee Valley Transportation Council, Whatcom County Council of Governments, and Yakima Valley Conference of Governments.

state's first acoustical barriers on I-405 to shield Bellevue neighborhoods from freeway noise. It also began building its first bicycle trails, and the Aeronautics Commission adopted the state's first comprehensive Airport System Plan.

Then Washington and the rest of the nation ran out of gas — literally.

In October 1973, the Arab-dominated Organization of Petroleum Exporting Countries stopped shipments to the United States in retaliation for its support of Israel in the Yom Kippur War. Gas prices soared, lines at service stations stretched for blocks, the federal government lowered interstate speed limits to 55 m.p.h., and just about everyone got the message that cars alone could no longer be relied on to meet society's transportation needs. Congress adopted the National Mass Transportation Act to increase transit system funding in 1974, and the State Highway Department joined with the Federal Highway Administration to write a new "Action Plan" for better coordination in addressing environmental, social, and economic impacts.

Coincidentally, the department finished its EIS for I-90 between Snoqualmie Pass and North Bend, and the federal courts allowed work to resume. Many more years would pass before construction could resume on the freeway's westernmost section.

Cancellation of Seattle's R. H. Thomson
Expressway left SR 520 "ramps to nowhere."

Bicycles and pedestrians also gained new respect, particularly in Seattle, which converted much of the former Seattle, Lake Shore & Eastern Railroad into the Burke-Gilman Trail. The "rail to trail" movement would gain adherents across the state, and bike and pedestrian lanes were soon incorporated into many new highway and bridge designs.

A Broader Vision

In the 1975 and 1976 Transportation Agencies Annual Reports, the Highway Department calculated that it had shed nearly 1,000 employees from a peak of 5,300 in 1970–1971, and projected that expenditures would decline by a fourth to $282 million in the coming biennium. In actuality, expenditures dropped even lower over the next two years due to declining state and federal revenues.

George Andrews decided to retire in late 1975, and was succeeded by William A. Bulley, who had served as a district engineer in the department since 1962. He had been a lead engineer on I-5's Ship Canal Bridge and in addressing the instability of Seattle's Capitol and Beacon hills as they were excavated for the new freeway. He helped the department arrive at the innovative solution of staggered ranks of "cylinder wall piles," later adopted by other highway builders.

Like Andrews, Bulley was a supporter of mass transit and other approaches to increasing the people-carrying capacity of existing highways. He later recalled, "We were a highway department but how long could we keep building new lanes? I truly felt we were running out of geography." Early on Bulley's watch, the Legislature authorized local and county governments to create "Public Transportation Benefit Areas" (PTBA) for funding and operating transit services. Snohomish County's Community Transit promptly organized in 1976, the first of 11 new PTBA agencies to form over the next five years.

Bulley's main focus remained completion of the state's planned 762 miles of interstate highways. More than 100 miles remained unfinished, most notably the final stretch of I-90 between I-405 and I-5, which was the Highway Commission's highest priority. Here, at last, some progress was made as Bulley took over the delicate negotiations with King County and the cities of Seattle, Bellevue, and Mercer Island on the highway's final design.

During years of discussion guided by George Andrews, the highway had steadily shrunk from its original 18-lane configuration to eight

Seattle opens the Burke-Gilman Trail, state's first pedestrian-bicycle path on a former railroad right of way, in 1974.

Federal injunction against construction of "North Bend Bypass" on I-90 is lifted in May 1974.

Legislature grants county and city officials authority to create Public Transportation Benefit Areas (PTBA), independent bodies to provide public transportation, in 1975.

William A. Bulley becomes Director of Highways on November 1, 1975.

Highway Commission signs a memorandum of understanding for a revised I-90 project with Seattle, Mercer Island, Bellevue, and King County on December 21, 1976.

— including two lanes reserved for buses and HOVs and future light rail — camouflaged with extensive landscaped lids in Seattle and on Mercer Island. The latter's mayor, Aubrey Davis (also chair of the Metro Transit committee and a future Transportation Commissioner) had famously said of I-90 that his community didn't want to "see it, hear it, or smell it."

Final agreement was close on outstanding issues of scale and local access. Representatives of Bellevue, Mercer Island, Seattle, King County, and the Highway Department sat down for a marathon session mediated by Jerry Cormick in December

Metro chair C. Cary Donworth shows Senator Magnuson a model of an articulated bus, ca. 1975. Below: Dixy Lee Ray 1976 campaign brochure.

1976. While reporters and TV crews hovered, they hammered out a final "3-2T-3" configuration for six general traffic lanes and two dedicated transit lanes. All parties signed the memorandum of understanding on December 21, 1976, but the war was far from over.

In January 1977, Washington's first woman governor, Dixy Lee Ray, took office. A marine biologist, first director of the Pacific Science Center, and controversial member of the Atomic Energy Commission, Ray had never held an elected post before. Her "inexperience" may have helped her cut the Gordian knot that had held up creation of a State Transportation Department.

The new department consolidated the Department of Highways, Toll Bridge Authority, Aeronautics Commission, Canal Commission, and some functions of several other agencies. Governor Ray accepted the Legislature's view that the new department should be as insulated from politics as possible. It would

be guided by a seven-member Transportation Commission, four of whom would reside west of the Cascades and three of whom would live on the east; no more than four members could belong to the same political party. This body, and this body alone, would select the Secretary of Transportation, who would serve until and unless dismissed for cause (which did not prevent Governor Ray from promoting her own candidate, Aubrey Davis, to run the agency).

"With no fuss or fanfare," according to *The Seattle Times*, the new Transportation Commission held its first

Eleven-mile section of I-205 bypassing Vancouver opens to traffic on December 22, 1976.

Department introduces "value engineering" in its I-90 design work in 1977.

President Carter names Seattle Congressman Brock Adams as U.S. Secretary of Transportation in 1977.

Lynda Wheeler becomes WSF's first female deck officer on July 3, 1977.

State concepts for massive I-90 trenches through Seattle and Mercer Island sparked local opposition.

meeting on September 21, 1977. Its initial membership was carried over from the Highway Commission: former Congresswoman Julia Butler Hansen of Cathlamet, Ray Aardal of Bremerton, Seattle's Virginia Gunby, Ellensburg's Howard Sorensen, and James Swinyard from Deer Park. (Governor Ray would later appoint Robert Mikalson from Centralia and Vaughn Hubbard from Waitsburg.) Their first act was to name William Bulley as acting Secretary of Transportation, a compromise with the governor, followed by approval of a $401 million budget for 1979–1981.

Virginia Gunby cast the sole "nay" on the budget. She was also a leader in the campaign for Initiative 348, which sought to repeal the state's new "variable" gas tax. Adopted in June, the law raised the gas tax from 9 to 11 cents immediately, and then allowed it to "float" with need up to 12 cents. It was premised on the inflated post-embargo gas prices, which later proved to be a shaky foundation, and transportation reformers preferred revenue sources that could support more than just highways. Indeed, Governor Evans had vetoed the first version of the variable gas-tax bill while trying to win approval of a Department of Transportation.

I-348 was a baptism by fire for the new commission and department. It also helped to rearrange the state's feuding transportation interests into some unusual new coalitions. The pro-348 cause attracted anti-highway liberals such as Gunby and anti-tax conservatives led by King County Assessor Harley Hoppe. The anti-348 cause put highway interests and transit systems on the same bus, along with downtown business interests, farmers, and rural towns.

Opponents of I-348 outspent its proponents by nearly 10 to one, but the vote on November 8, 1977, was too close to call. After a long, statewide recount, the repeal fell just 848 votes short of victory.

The new Department of Transportation was out of the garage, and it had some gas in the tank, but a very bumpy road lay ahead.

First demonstration project contract for recycling asphalt pavement begins in July 1977.

New Washington State Department of Transportation, guided by a new Transportation Commission, formally begins operation on September 21, 1977. The commission names William A. Bulley as the first Secretary of Transportation.

Initiative 348 to repeal variable gas tax adopted in June narrowly fails on November 8, 1977.

WSF Jumbo Mark II ferries Tacoma, Puyallup, *and* Wenatchee *were launched in the late 1990s.*

1978~2000: Changing Course

Locally built, innovative cable-stayed Intercity Bridge (now Ed Hendler Bridge) opens between Pasco and Kennewick in September 1978.

North Bend stages mock "funeral" for the last stop light on I-90 on October 13, 1978.

In the first railroad line rehabilitation project in the West, WSDOT starts work on a 61-mile spur line between Metaline Falls and Newport in 1979.

Metro Transit, King County, and City of Seattle establish nation's first public "vanpool" program in 1979.

The new Department of Transportation could not have been born in a more troubled time. Relations quickly soured between Governor Dixy Lee Ray and the press, U.S. Senator Warren G. Magnuson, and the Democratic leadership of the Legislature — most of whom would be swept away by voters or scandal by the end of 1980. Record interest rates combined with a national recession to produce "stagflation," driving up project costs while depressing state revenues. At least WSDOT had a friend in Washington, D.C., Secretary of Transportation and former Seattle Congressman Brock Adams, but the same economic forces were also squeezing federal resources.

The department's payroll had dropped below 4,000 in 1976. Most remaining work on I-90 west of the Cascades remained stalled by legal challenges, although the town of North Bend would officially

retire the last stop light on the route in October 1978. Progress was maintained elsewhere with the opening of the innovative Intercity (now Ed Hendler) Bridge between Pasco and Kennewick. This locally managed project, the first major cable-stayed bridge in the United States, replaced a 1922-vintage span in September 1978, and was later taken over by WSDOT.

Under pressure from the Legislature, the Transportation Commission sought a local shipyard for construction of six new 100-vehicle ferries. The contract was awarded to Marine Power & Equipment of Seattle, after the Legislature waived customary performance bond requirements. The new class was named after the first vessel launched, the *Issaquah*, which would feature computerized control systems. It was also the department's first experience with a "design-and-build" contract, but work on vital components was distributed among several subcontractors. This proved to be a recipe for confusion and later conflict

On June 11, 1978, a wayward freighter rammed Seattle's Spokane Street Bridge on the Duwamish River, jamming half the draw span in an upright position. Chief responsibility for its replacement fell on the City of Seattle, and construction was delayed by a kickback scandal that ultimately landed the City Engineer and several powerful legislators in prison. The U.S. Army Corps of Engineers finished a new high-level bridge in 1984, and the City later reconnected Harbor Island and West Seattle with a new swivel bridge. The majority of the replacement cost was covered by the federal government, thanks, once again, to the advocacy of Senator Magnuson.

The State might have played a larger role in the West Seattle project were it not struck by its own disaster on February 13, 1979, when the western half of the Hood

Completed in 1978, Pasco-Kennewick's Ed Hendler Intercity Bridge won national honors.

Canal Bridge sank in a "hundred-year storm." Ferries were pressed into duty, including the first service between Port Townsend and greater Seattle in four decades, and construction of new pontoons was rushed forward.

A happier occasion followed on June 22, 1979, when tolls were removed from the Evergreen Point Floating Bridge, and champagne flowed on August 24 with the lifting of the final federal injunction blocking construction of Interstate 90. (Unfortunately, financial shortfalls and political wrangling delayed resumption of major construction until 1983.)

Western half of Hood Canal Floating Bridge sinks in a storm on February 13, 1979. WSF provides ferry service until replacement is ready.

Federal courts lift injunction on final I-90 construction between Seattle and I-405 on August 24, 1979.

In its 1979 report to the Legislature, the Transportation Commission declared that it was fully engaged in development of "a comprehensive and balanced multi-modal transportation system." Just 11 percent of 764 miles of planned interstate highways remained to be completed, 18 emergency airfields were in operation, seven new Park and Ride lots were serving metropolitan Seattle commuters, and the department had secured its first funding for railroad line rehabilitation, making improvements to a 61-mile spur line between Metaline Falls and Newport in cooperation with the Pend Oreille Port District.

Looking west on the Hood Canal Bridge, February 13, 1979.

Stirred and Shaken

On April 7, 1980, Washington State Ferries employees walked off the job to demand higher wages and benefits, idling all but two of the 19-boat fleet. A new "Mosquito Fleet" of private craft, including the venerable *Virginia V*, was quickly mustered to maintain service while the commission and unions battled in the courts and at the negotiating table. The unions won most of their economic demands with a new contract on April 16, but the State won greater control over work rules and procedures. Commuters got their boats back, but at the price of an immediate 25 percent fare hike.

The State took possession of the new *Issaquah* ferry on July 1, 1980, and the vessel developed problems almost immediately. The day before her first public

The Issaquah *at Colman Dock.*

run, her engine broke down, and on her official July 14 debut, a lifeboat davit snapped, striking a Coast Guard inspector and narrowly missing several crewmen. It was only the beginning of a string of mechanical and electronic malfunctions that would plague the *Issaquah* and her sister ships for years to come and lead to costly repairs and lawsuits.

There was no refuge on dry land, either. On May 18, 1980, at 8:32 a.m., Mount St. Helens' cataclysmic eruption instantly scoured 200 square miles of forest — and 30 miles of SR 504 — with boiling gas and mud, killing 57 people and spreading a choking cloud of ash over most of Eastern and Southwestern Washington. More than 1,000 miles of state highways and roads had to be closed, some for months, and repairs ran into the hundreds of millions of dollars. President Jimmy Carter and Senator Warren Magnuson responded quickly with emergency aid, which, however, did nothing to save their careers.

The "Reagan Revolution" of 1980 was the political equivalent of Mount St. Helens' eruption, a tectonic shift

William Bulley

William Arthur Bulley, the final Director of Highways (1975–1977), became the first Secretary of Transportation (1977–1981) after department reorganization into the current Washington State Department of Transportation (WSDOT).

Born in Spokane in 1925, Bulley served in the Army in Europe during World War II. After graduation from the University of Washington, he began working for the State Highway Department as a bridge engineer, quickly moving up in the department holding various district engineer titles. In his first department position, he was in charge of Seattle freeway bridges, including the Ship Canal Bridge. Later he became heavily involved in the construction of Interstate 5 through Seattle, using the new and unique design of "cylinder wall piles" to shore up the east hills when during construction they began sliding.

Bulley headed the department during the sinking of the Hood Canal Bridge, difficult labor troubles within the ferry system, and the eruption of Mount St. Helens that destroyed more than 30 miles of State Route 504 and temporarily closed more than 1,000 miles of state highways along with I-90 and I-405. In his words, these were "very expensive troubles," but he was happy to be able to find solutions to get everything resolved. He is most proud of the memorandum of understanding with Seattle, Mercer Island, Bellevue, and King County that allowed the I-90 project to win federal approval and enabled its construction to be completed after many years in limbo.

After a 30-year career with the department, Bulley retired in 1981 and began working for H. W. Lochner, a Chicago transportation planning and engineering company with offices in Bellevue.

DUANE BERENTSON

Duane Berentson, born in 1928, spent 18 years representing Burlington, Skagit County, in the State House of Representatives following his election in 1962. He served on the House Transportation Committee for almost his entire tenure and helped to pass enabling legislation for public transportation. Named Republican co-Speaker of the House in 1979, he was a candidate for governor in 1980. Berentson was appointed Secretary of Transportation in 1981, and was the first non-engineer to serve as chief executive of Washington's highway transportation program. He retired in 1993.

As Secretary of Transportation, Berentson continued to broaden the Department of Transportation's highway and road-building focus to include mass transportation. He is credited with instilling a new sense of purpose and professionalism in the department. He established better communication with, and better effort from, the Legislature for the department. However, he was beset by the woes of the troubled Issaquah class of ferries, and by labor issues and harassment lawsuits within Washington State Ferries. Ferry workers struck on his first day in the position.

Interstate 90 was completed through the state during Berentson's watch. He negotiated final federal funding for I-90 and secured federal funding to complete U.S. 395 to the Tri-Cities. In 1990, the Downtown Seattle Transit Tunnel was finished, and the Legislature approved the High Capacity Transit Act, paving the way for a regional mass transportation system to be studied. Although an accident sank the first Lake Washington Floating Bridge (the Lacey V. Murrow Bridge) later in 1990, the Homer M. Hadley Floating Bridge next to it had been completed the year before (the replacement bridge was opened in 1993). Berentson summed up his tenure: "I came in at a controversial time. There were several incidents, but it all worked out. The ferries that were delivered still function today."

in national politics that would permanently alter the relationship between states and the national government, increasing local discretion while reducing federal aid relative to its historical levels. State Attorney General Slade Gorton defeated Senator Magnuson and Governor John Spellman replaced Dixy Lee Ray as Republicans took control of the Legislature. William Bulley retired in 1981, and the Transportation Commission named Duane Berentson to succeed him on May 21, 1981.

The former co-Speaker of the House of Representatives was the first non-engineer to lead the State's transportation program. He encountered some resistance in a department long dominated by technocrats. As he later recalled, "I told them I wouldn't pretend to be an engineer if they wouldn't pretend to be administrators."

Berentson's tenure began with dedication of the Denny Creek Bridge on I-90 just west of the Snoqualmie Pass summit on July 30, 1981, and two months later the

Building I-182's Lee and Volpentest bridges.

Denny Creek Bridge on I-90.

department introduced its first on-ramp meters on I-5. Although the State's original portion of the interstate system was years from completion, it now faced a growing maintenance backlog for existing highways and roads. The Legislature abandoned its controversial variable gas-tax rate in favor of a flat 10 percent based on average statewide retail prices, which provided more funding in the short term, and department engineers instituted a computerized pavement management system to schedule resurfacing work more efficiently.

There were other improvements. Highway lighting was converted to more efficient bulbs to reduce costs. Community groups and volunteers helped collect litter along state roads through the "Adopt-a-Highway" program.

The department's role in rail service expanded with the bankruptcy of the Milwaukee Road, which had served many rural communities and farms in Central and Eastern Washington. Tracks were upgraded and services maintained with the aid of $5.3 million in federal funds and, later, local and state matching dollars. WSDOT opened discussions with the beleaguered Amtrak system to explore similar partnerships to maintain and possibly expand passenger rail services. In other examples of rail's revival, Seattle proudly unveiled its Waterfront Streetcar

Mount St. Helens erupts on May 18, 1980, wiping out much of SR 504 and temporarily closing more than 1,000 miles of state highways.

The *Issaquah*, first of a controversial new class of ferry, is launched in Tacoma on December 29, 1980.

Washington's population passes 4,132,400 in 1980.

Duane Berentson becomes second Secretary of Transportation on May 21, 1981.

Denny Creek Bridge on I-90 is dedicated on July 30, 1981.

First "FLOW" on-ramp meters with stop lights to regulate the flow of traffic onto I-5 are installed on September 30, 1981.

Legislature opens the shoulders of most limited-access highways and freeways to bicycles in March 1982.

Building the I-205 Glen Jackson Bridge (Jeremiah Coughlan, The Columbian).

in 1982 (eight years after the Yakima Valley Transportation Company had restored electric streetcar service between Yakima and Selah).

The year 1982 ended with two gratifying accomplishments: the opening of the replacement Hood Canal Bridge on October 3, and completion of the I-205 bridge between Vancouver and Portland, a joint project with the State of Oregon. The last of the Issaquah Class ferries, the *Sealth*, was launched in 1982, but this proved to be no cause for celebration as the State and Marine Power tangled over the vessel's seaworthiness.

The State did not take formal possession of the *Sealth* until October 3, 1983. The very next day, the Super Ferry *Elwha* ran aground near Orcas Island during an unauthorized "sightseeing cruise." WSF Director Nick Tracy was later removed amid growing staff turmoil, but he regained his former job as a ferryboat captain.

By 1983, WSDOT was facing serious shortfalls in funding for priority projects such Tacoma's I-705 spur, I-5 expansion in Olympia, and, of course, I-90. Washington was not alone, and contrary to its tax-cutting reputation, the Reagan Administration approved the first federal gas-tax increase since 1956. Similarly, the Legislature scrapped its average retail rate formula and levied a simple 16-cent-per-gallon tax, with a further two-cent rise set for July 1984. The new revenues helped to temporarily relieve the department's funding crisis and maintain construction.

Another milestone was passed on November 27, 1984, with the opening of twin bridges between Pasco and Richland on I-182. This spur on I-82 had been opposed by Yakima, Pendleton, and Portland, whose business interests feared it would siphon shoppers to the Tri-Cities, and by local environmentalists who battled the route in the courts from 1973 to 1980. The new bridges were named for *Tri-Cities Herald* publisher Glenn C. Lee and Benton-Franklin Good Roads Association leader Sam Volpentest, who persevered to see I-182's completion a quarter of a century after it was first proposed.

New Tools

A new governor, Booth Gardner, took office in January 1985, and the department moved to resolve its dispute with Marine Power & Equipment over the Issaquah Class ferries. The parties settled more than $60 million in suits and counter-suits on June 25.

In the mid-1980s, the department made steady gains in both new construction and maintenance of existing highways. With its new gas-tax revenues, WSDOT committed to resurfacing 1,200 miles of state roads each year through 1989. It also undertook repairs of dozens of bridges, upgrades of heavily used rural roads, and improvements such as HOV lanes and metered on-ramps to increase the capacity of urban highways. Engineering was expedited with the introduction of a "Transportation Information and Planning System" (TRIPS) to collect and disseminate data on road conditions and traffic patterns.

97

As work progressed on Lake Washington for the new I-90 floating bridge, Metro Transit went underground in 1987 to add another key link. The Downtown Seattle Transit Tunnel was designed mainly to funnel dual mode diesel-electric buses beneath city streets to and from I-5 and I-90, but its planners envisioned that it would ultimately carry interurban trains. The next year, the new State Convention & Trade Center opened on a lid spanning I-5 in downtown Seattle.

Also in 1988, King County voters overwhelmingly endorsed "accelerated" planning for a rail transit system, and the State initiated a study of potential high-speed "bullet train" routes. Development of any rail system depended on the Legislature, which was still wary of big-ticket transit projects. No one was quite prepared when in the waning days of the 1990 legislative

Mandatory use of seat belts takes effect on July 1, 1986.

Legislature creates High Speed Rail Commission to explore "bullet train" concepts in 1988.

The Spokane River Centennial Trail, a paved path along the river from the Idaho state line to Nine Mile Falls, opens in 1989.

State Commission for Efficiency and Accountability in Government recommends 38 discrete reforms and improvements in WSDOT in 1989.

Third floating bridge across Lake Washington (later named for Homer M. Hadley) opens on June 4, 1989.

Washington State and federally recognized Indian tribes in Washington sign "Centennial Accord" for greater cooperation on August 4, 1989.

Restoration of the historic 1905 covered bridge over Grays River in Wahkiakum County is completed on September 28, 1989.

First guidelines for management and treatment of highway storm water are proposed in October 1989.

The Downtown Seattle Transit Tunnel opened in September 1990.

Timeline

Washington celebrates the centennial of its statehood on November 11, 1989.

Legislature enacts High Capacity Transportation Act and Growth Management Act in spring 1990.

Mandatory driver's liability insurance takes effect on July 1, 1990.

While under reconstruction, the original 1940 Lacey V. Murrow Floating Bridge sinks during a violent storm on November 25, 1990.

Washington's population tops 4,866,700 in 1990.

session, House Transportation Committee chair Ruth Fisher hammered together a compromise to authorize a Regional Transit Planning Authority for Puget Sound. More astounding still, House Speaker Joe King shepherded a Growth Management Act to passage in the same session. Suddenly, transit advocates and urban planners had the long-sought ability to coordinate transportation policy and land use development.

Any elation at King County's Metro Transit was short-lived. On September 6, 1990, Federal Judge William Dwyer ruled that the municipal utility's council of local government officials violated the constitution's standard for equal representation. A week later, Metro opened the downtown transit tunnel. In 1994 King County would absorb the agency.

The year would end badly for WSDOT as well. A sudden storm flooded the pontoons of the original Lake Washington floating bridge, then under reconstruction, and sent them to the bottom on November 25, 1990. Fortunately the new parallel floating bridge (subsequently named for Homer M. Hadley) had opened the previous year, and traffic was already using it.

The following year, the ferry system was roiled by new charges of racial and sexual harassment. Thomas F. Heinan succeeded Admiral Howard Parker as WSF manager, with the mission of calming the waters, but he lasted only two years. Former United Airlines executive Paul Green took the helm in 1993 and his mantra of "safety, schedule, and service" helped to reform and stabilize the system's labor relations and business practices.

Toutle River and SR 504 after the 1980 eruption.
Upper right: Grays River covered bridge before restoration.

I-90's Mercer Island lid, ca. 1990. Inset: Lake Washigton Floating Bridge sinking.

The workplace tensions belied — or reflected — the advances WSDOT had made over the past decade to integrate its workforce, promote women, and boost the share of contracts awarded to businesses owned by minorities and women (more than 11 percent of total awards by 1990). Labor relations were also complicated by implementation of internal reforms proposed by a special State Commission for Efficiency and Accountability.

In December 1991, President George H. W. Bush signed the Intermodal Surface Transportation Efficiency Act, or ISTEA (pronounced "Ice Tea" by planners), to fund and promote mass transit, bicycles, pedestrian trails, HOV lanes, and other modes of transportation beyond the automobile. The State followed up with a "Commuter Trip Reduction Act" to encourage employers to provide alternative means of transportation such as car and van pools, bus passes, and even telecommuting for their workforces.

The last full year of Duane Berentson's tenure saw the opening of the first segment of Mount St. Helens' Spirit Lake Memorial Highway and WSDOT's purchase of the 20-mile Toppenish-White Swan railroad. Berentson took a well-deserved retirement at the end of May 1993 and was succeeded by former Republican Congressman Sid Morrison on June 1. (The SR 20 Swinomish Channel Bridge was later dedicated in Berentson's honor.)

By then, Governor Mike Lowry had taken office. He reappointed the incumbent members of the Transportation Commission, whose confirmations had been delayed through the campaign season, and added the name of Lawrence Weldon, a Teamster official and the commission's first African American member. Lowry strongly supported the commission's appointment of Sid Morrison, even though Morrison had been a candidate for the Republican nomination for governor the previous year.

President George H. W. Bush signs the Intermodal Surface Transportation Efficiency Act (ISTEA) on December 18, 1991.

First section of the Spirit Lake Memorial Highway (SR 504) at Mt. St. Helens opens on October 16, 1992.

WSDOT purchases the 20-mile Toppenish-White Swan rail line in 1993.

Legislature approves the New Partners: Public Private Initiatives in Transportation Program in 1993.

WSDOT, University of Washington, and Washington State University establish the Washington State Transportation Center (TRAC) to undertake joint research projects in 1993.

AMTRAK Cascades. Lower left: Lawrence Weldon, first African American WSTC member. Lower right: Aubrey Davis and friend opening I-90 in 1993.

Lowry and Morrison could find little traction in the Legislature to apply the state sales tax to fuel (which also avoided the restrictions under Amendment 18), but they did win passage of the "New Partners" program to test the willingness of private enterprise to undertake transportation improvements in exchange for toll revenues and other potential income. Fourteen proposals would be submitted by the 1994 deadline for evaluation by Jerry Ellis and her staff. Most withered under fiscal scrutiny or public opposition and only one — the new Tacoma Narrows Bridge — ultimately saw the light of day, but not without a struggle.

Moving Right Along

During Morrison's first year, the department acted on a citizen suggestion and authorized the posting of signs on state roads to memorialize victims of drunk drivers. It also officially named the new Lake Washington Floating Bridge in honor of pioneering engineer Homer M. Hadley. On November 1, 1993, Skagit County voters approved the state's latest Public Transportation Benefit Authority, SKAT, on the fourth try. Voters statewide endorsed Initiative 601, a cap on the growth of state spending that would squeeze future funding for transportation.

In 1994, Washington received its final allocation under the original 1956 Interstate and Defense Highway program, which had been repeatedly renewed and expanded. Federal grants shifted

Sid Morrison becomes third Secretary of Transportation on June 1, 1993.

Completion of I-90 is celebrated in Seattle on September 12, 1993.

Placement of DUI victim memorial signs begins in fall 1993.

WSDOT's Aviation Division wins national praise in 1994 for its Rural Emergency Medical Service Lighting Program.

Washington's first state-funded passenger train departs Seattle's King Street Station for Portland on April 1, 1994.

to more flexible formulas for both highway and transit projects. At the same time, Secretary Morrison reorganized the department into major "customer-centered groups," while giving regional highway administrators greater responsibility and autonomy (and hiring the first non-engineer, John Okamoto, to run a region). He divided policy and operations between two deputy secretaries, Gretchen White and Stan Moon respectively.

Also in 1994, WSDOT launched its pilot website — a radical innovation back then — and the Aviation Division earned top national honors for its program to light emergency helicopter pads at rural hospitals.

On April 1 (a dangerous day to start any new venture), the department joined with Amtrak and the State of Oregon to inaugurate a six-month demonstration of Seattle-Portland rail service using new "Talgo" trains from Spain. Contrary to superstition, the sleek trains with their distinctive fifties-style tailfins were an instant hit. Daily round-trip service began the next year between Seattle and Vancouver, B.C., the beginning of today's popular "Cascades" runs. On the far side of the state, WSDOT's new "Grain Trains" began operating in and out of the Port of Walla Walla in the fall of 1994.

The Washington State Transportation Commission was the prime backer of WSDOT's expanding role in rail services. "We were becoming a real transportation commission, not just a bigger highway board," recalls Aubrey Davis, who joined the commission

SID MORRISON

Sid Morrison was born in 1933 and grew up in Zillah, Washington, on a family orchard pioneered by his grandfather. He was elected to the Washington State House of Representatives in 1967, and became a state senator representing Yakima in 1974. In 1980, he was elected to the U.S. House of Representatives for the 4th Congressional District, and concentrated his efforts on forestry, energy projects, and environmental concerns. Morrison was appointed Secretary of Transportation in 1993 and retired in 2001.

As Secretary of Transportation, Morrison made a sweeping agency-wide reorganization to shift the department from its highway and road focus to assume a greater role in freight and passenger rail, aviation, ferries, bicycles, and mass-transit — moves begun in the department by predecessors George Andrews, William Bulley, and Duane Berentson. In his reorganization, Morrison tried to do away with the department hierarchy to give employees more decision-making power and to increase department efficiency with the reduction of paperwork and bureaucracy. Compressed workweeks, flextime, and telecommuting became much more widely used during his tenure, and in 2000 WSDOT had the lowest employee turnover of any state agency.

During Morrison's time as head of the department, voters in seven counties gave the go-ahead for the second Tacoma Narrows Bridge, and state voters passed Referendum 49 to fund $2.3 billion in transportation projects while reducing the MVET (effectively reversed by passage of Initiative 695 a year later). Also on Morrison's watch, the state expanded bike lanes (below) and introduced "Grain Trains" and "Cascades" passenger service.

Tacoma's I-705 Spur and the 1997 cable-stayed bridge over Thea Foss Waterway.

WSDOT launches its first website in July 1994.

A major departmental reorganization takes effect on July 1, 1994.

WSDOT inaugurates its first "Grain Train," with six rail cars operating out of the Port of Walla Walla, in fall 1994.

Clark County voters reject a plan to extend Portland, Oregon's popular MAX light rail system north of the Columbia River on February 7, 1995.

King, Pierce, and Snohomish counties reject a proposed $6.7 billion Regional Transit Authority plan on March 14, 1995.

With WSDOT funding, daily rail service between Seattle and Vancouver, B.C., resumes after a 14-year hiatus in May 1995.

WSDOT makes first use of new "hot-in-place" asphalt recycling in Yakima County in July 1995.

in 1992 and chaired it between 1994 and 1995. The commission also launched an ambitious citizen outreach effort to engage local communities in prioritizing their needs — and then figuring out how to pay for them. "We made citizens do what governors and legislators have to do every session and balance revenues and project expenditures," Davis says.

Despite the success of the Talgo service and the Transportation Commission's outreach efforts, 1995 was a disappointing year. The Legislature again balked at any substantial revenue increases (and actually cut the WSDOT budget). Clark County voters firmly rejected a proposal to extend metropolitan Portland's "MAX" light rail line to Vancouver, and Puget Sound voters turned down a $6.7 billion regional transit plan. Grant County had better luck with a demonstration of its proposed Public Transportation Benefit Authority, which voters approved in 1996.

In November 1995, President Bill Clinton signed the National Highway System Act, allocating $6 billion in new funds. The law also lifted the national 55 m.p.h. speed limit on interstate highways, which had been imposed in response to the 1973–1974 OPEC oil embargo. Washington began adjusting its speed limits the following March.

In February 1996, storms washed away the SR 12 bridge across the Naches River and caused more than $60 million in damage to state roads. John Conrad, then Assistant Secretary for Field Operations, lamented, "We had so many roads closed we ran out of 'Road Closed' signs."

Then even as the state dried out, the following month reaffirmed that the road to a very hot place can be paved with good intentions. Amid high hopes in late 1995, the department began experimenting with light fill material made from shredded tires to solve persistent slide problems on some routes in Pacific County. In March 1996, SR 100 near Ilwaco began to radiate heat and emit a rank odor — and then burst into flames. WSDOT promptly scrapped the recycling program.

That spring, the Transportation Commission adopted its first 20-year comprehensive plan for all forms of surface transportation in the state. The effort represented collaboration with local governments and agencies, and included input from nearly 6,000 citizens. WSDOT also joined with the Puget Sound Regional Council, port districts, local governments, and private groups to form "FAST" (Freight Action Strategy for Seattle-Tacoma-Everett) to address ways to expedite the flow of cargo and freight in central Puget Sound.

Washington State Ferries launched its largest ferry yet on August 29, 1996, the Jumbo Mark II Class *Tacoma* (followed by the *Wenatchee* in 1997 and the *Puyallup* in 1999). The *Tacoma's* early propulsion troubles felt like Issaquah Class deja vu, but in due time the kinks were worked out.

On November 5, 1996, the voters of King, Pierce, and Snohomish counties approved a scaled-back $3.9 billion "Sound Transit" plan for new light and commuter rail services and express buses. The plan included expanded HOV lanes and Park and Ride terminals in partnership with WSDOT. The plan's adoption culminated a campaign for rail transit that had begun in 1958 and persevered through four subsequent election defeats.

The following month, WSDOT inaugurated its Rideshare program with transit agencies in Thurston, Pierce, King, Kitsap, and Snohomish counties. The service matches commuting drivers and passengers, and helps to increase use of HOV lanes in the Puget Sound region.

Demonstration transit service begins in Grant County on November 1, 1995, and voters fund permanent system one year later.

Federal government lifts national 55 m.p.h. limit on December 8, 1995, and Washington raises limits the following March.

Transportation Commission adopts its first 20-year surface transportation plan in spring 1996.

WSDOT and Puget Sound Regional Council join with port districts, local governments, and private groups to form "FAST" (Freight Action Strategy for Seattle-Tacoma-Everett) partnership in 1996.

WSF launches its first Jumbo Mark II ferry, the *Tacoma*, on August 29, 1996.

King, Pierce, and Snohomish County voters approve revised $3.9 billion "Sound Transit" plan on November 5, 1996.

Rideshare program, coordinated by WSDOT and local transit authorities, begins in Thurston, Pierce, King, Kitsap, and Snohomish counties in December 1996.

Medivac helicopters at WSDOT airfield.

WSF passenger ferry Chinook.

104

Gary Locke took office as the nation's first Chinese American governor in January 1997, in time for two long-awaited ribbon cutting ceremonies. First, the dramatic and beautiful SR 509 cable-stayed bridge opened on January 22 over Tacoma's Thea Foss Waterway, bringing completion to the I-705 spur and further boosting downtown Tacoma's dramatic revival. Next came the dedication of Mount St. Helens' new Johnston Ridge Observatory and the final segment of SR 504 on May 21.

Sticker Shocks

In the fall of 1997, the department joined with the Washington State Patrol to address "high accident locations" on state highways through a combination of engineering improvements and intensified enforcement. The effort yielded almost immediate results by cutting collisions on one notorious stretch of I-5 in north Seattle by more than two thirds. The Transportation Commission also called for changes in driver education to respond to the rising number of "road rage" incidents, and the State Patrol organized special Aggressive Driver Apprehension Teams the following July.

In 1998, the Transportation Commission adopted a new Aviation Policy to preserve existing airfields, improve flight safety, and ensure capacity. The State was also a participant in the long effort to address the future capacity needs of Seattle-Tacoma International Airport. After exhausting other alternatives, the Puget Sound Regional Council had concluded in 1992 that Sea-Tac needed to add a controversial third runway. Legal challenges delayed the project until 2004.

Washington State Ferries launched its first passenger-only ferry, the catamaran *Chinook*, on May 15, 1998, and inaugurated service between Colman Dock and Bremerton (suspended in 2003 due to budget issues and complaints from waterfront owners in Rich Passage). That same month, the department convened the first national conference on "car-sharing," i.e., use of designated automobiles by multiple drivers, reviving an idea first promulgated in the 1930s by Technocracy, Inc. The conference led indirectly to the formation of FlexCar, a private membership organization, a few years later.

Transportation dominated the 1998 session of the Legislature and pitted Governor Locke and fellow Democrats against Republicans who narrowly controlled the State House. The latter declined to support additional funding for transportation without reforms to improve WSDOT's "efficiency" and "accountability." Locke agreed to formation of a Blue Ribbon Commission on Transportation to make long-term recommendations and, it was hoped, lay the roadbed for a statewide consensus to support future transportation funding.

This body brought together 47 representatives of transportation agencies, organizations, companies, and other constituencies to evaluate the present condition and needs of the state's transportation system and how it is administered, and to lay out a 20-year plan for its improvement. Boeing executive Doug Bieghle served as its chair, and Kjris Lund guided its public outreach, research, and deliberations as staff director.

In the same legislative session, Referendum 49 was approved for place-ment on the November 1998 ballot. The proposal trimmed license tab fees while authorizing $1.9 billion in bonds for unspecified highway improvements to be underwritten through a reallocation of state revenues. The governor and most Democrats condemned the proposal as "credit card government," but taxpayers apparently preferred to pocket the imme-diate savings and approved the measure. This was the first in a string of bitter political and legal battles over the MVET.

Working on the Railroad

In the early 1990s, a national shortage of rail hopper cars made it difficult and expensive for Washington state farmers to get wheat and barley to market. The transcontinental railroads were earning more money hauling grain from the Midwest to ports in the Pacific Northwest than they could through shorter-distance trips within Washington. Empty grain cars for Eastern Washington grain shippers were in short supply.

To help alleviate this shortage, in 1994 WSDOT and the Washington State Energy Office purchased and repaired 29 used grain cars to collect wheat and barley from grain elevators throughout southeast Washington and haul it to grain export facilities in deepwater ports along the Columbia River and Puget Sound, where grain is loaded onto ships bound for Pacific Rim markets.

The first "Washington Grain Train" was a joint effort among the Port of Walla Walla, WSDOT, the Blue Mountain Railroad, and four Walla Walla area grain co-ops. The $763,000 needed to purchase the original 29 cars came from successful litigation against oil companies that had overcharged farmers during the 1970s. Once the trains were in service, their income was used to acquire an additional 65 rail cars and to expand the service area into 13 communities in Whitman, Grant, and Adams counties, at no cost to taxpayers.

SR 504 bridge near Mount St. Helens.

On November 18, Secretary Morrison announced the approval of a $350 million private partnership plan for a new Tacoma Narrows Bridge. Three weeks later, volunteers towed the rusting hulk of the former State ferry *Kalakala* into Elliott Bay, but to date hopes for her restoration have foundered.

On January 11, 1999, Amtrak formally inaugurated "Cascades" rail service between Eugene, Portland, and Seattle, with three Talgo trains, two of them purchased by WSDOT. A fourth Talgo joined the route in September.

In June, WSDOT engineers gently relocated the Dosewallips River Bridge on US 101 using giant "roller skates." The move preserved service on the bridge while a new span was built along side it. The technique was used again in 2003 to expand Bellevue's 8th Street Bridge over I-405.

State and local agencies celebrated the 20th anniversary of the nation's oldest van pooling program, begun in King County, on October 27, but there was no merriment a week later when voters okayed Initiative 695. Organized by conservative populist Tim Eyman, and chiefly financed by auto dealers, the initiative proposed to limit annual MVET to a flat $30, slashing revenues for highways, ferries, transit systems, and local governments by an estimated $750 million a year.

The State Supreme Court voided the measure for multiple constitutional defects a year later — after the Legislature had already adopted a flat $30 fee while permitting local option increases for projects such as Sound Transit and Seattle's monorail expansion. Adoption of the new MVET erased the $2 billion-plus in new transportation funding authorized by Referendum 49 just one year earlier.

During 2000, the department undertook a number of new programs to expedite highway traffic flows and improve safety. In February, it began posting signs urging motorists involved in minor accidents to move their cars to the shoulder, and in July it joined with the State Patrol and the Tow Truck Association to

State voters pass Referendum 49, which reduces MVET, reallocates funds, and authorizes $2.3 billion in transportation projects, on November 3, 1998.

WSDOT approves a $350 million "transportation-partnership" proposal to build a new toll bridge across the Tacoma Narrows on November 18, 1998.

Local enthusiasts return *Kalakala* to Seattle on December 6, 1998, but restoration plans are later scuttled.

With WSDOT funding and aid, Amtrak inaugurates "Cascades" service between Eugene, Portland, and Seattle on January 11, 1999.

The U.S. Department of the Interior lists nine Pacific Northwest salmon runs as "endangered species" on March 16, 1999.

The Sequim Bypass on U.S. 101 opens on August 18, 1999.

Voters approve Initiative 695, capping annual MVET at $30, on November 2, 1999. The Supreme Court later voids the initiative, but the Legislature enacts the MVET cap.

WSDOT inaugurates the Moses Lake Grain Train on April 21, 2000.

Historic Dosewallips River Bridge was repositioned in 2003. Below: Sound Transit's "Sounder" commuter train (Sound Transit).

deploy "service patrols" on heavily used portions of I-5.

The I-90 Park Road Bridge opened in Spokane on October 6, 2000, marking the first significant highway expansion in the Spokane Valley since the 1950s. Work to separate the dangerous intersection of SR 17 and SR 26 near Othello also began late that year. The last year of the twentieth century saw something of a rebirth of a nineteenth-century technology as Sound Transit inaugurated its first "Sounder" commuter trains between Seattle and Tacoma. Also, WSDOT's second "Grain Train" began serving Moses Lake.

The most important advance came on November 29, 2000, with release of the Blue Ribbon Commission on Transportation's final report. It outlined an ambitious set of governance reforms, administrative and programmatic changes to enhance accountability, and funding strategies that would set the department's agenda in 2001 and beyond. It also surveyed a deep and broad chasm between state transportation revenues and future needs.

107

WSDOT, Washington State Patrol, and Tow Truck Association launch Service Patrols on I-5 in July 2000.

Sound Transit inaugurates "Sounder" commuter rail service between Tacoma and Seattle on September 18, 2000. (Service is extended to Everett in September 2003.)

Park Road Bridge opens in Spokane Valley, marking completion of several major I-90 improvements, on October 6, 2000.

Blue Ribbon Commission on Transportation issues its final report on November 29, 2000.

Washington's population reaches 5,894,121 in 2000.

Computer-generated illustration of new (left) and old Tacoma Narrows bridges.

A New Century: 2001 and Beyond

WSDOT aids Yakama Indian Nation with a rail spur for its new sawmill in 2001.

A severe earthquake near Olympia causes more than $1 billion in damage to roads and infrastructure on February 28, 2001. WSDOT inspects 1,456 affected bridges and elevated structures, including Seattle's Alaskan Way Viaduct.

The final report of the Blue Ribbon Commission on Transportation warned, "Washington's transportation system is on a collision course with reality." This would prove to be prophetic in more ways than one as the first year of the new millennium began.

Steering the department through the obstacles to come would fall to a new director, Douglas B. MacDonald, a Washington native and lawyer who had spent much of his professional career managing mega-projects such as the cleanup of Boston Harbor. Sid Morrison had signalled his desire to depart in fall 2000 and both the Transportation Commission and Governor Gary Locke agreed that MacDonald's record of accomplishment and philosophy of public accountability made him the ideal successor to restablish momentum at and confidence in the Washington State Department of Transportation.

MacDonald formally took charge of WSDOT on April 23, 2001, which was also the last day of a stormy regular Legislative session complicated by a partisan tie in the House and a slim Democratic majority in the Senate. Governor Locke had proposed a $17.2 billion transportation package based on the Blue Ribbon Commission's "Early Action Plan." He also sought appointing authority over the Secretary of Transportation. The Legislature stalemated on both requests.

Governor Gary Locke

Amid these deliberations, shortly before 11 a.m. on Ash Wednesday, February 28, 2001, the earth shuddered beneath the Nisqually Delta, toppling brick façades from Olympia to Seattle and damaging roads and public infrastructure throughout Western Washington. WSDOT engineers quickly inspected nearly 1,500 bridges in the quake zone, paying particular attention to Seattle's aging Alaskan Way Viaduct, and reopened most routes within days of the temblor, which registered 6.8 on the Richter Scale.

Governor Locke summoned the Legislature back to Olympia in late April for the first of three special sessions focusing on the transportation budget — with no better result. At the end of the last session on July 25, the usually soft-spoken Locke blasted opponents of his transportation plan in a radio interview. It would take a while for tempers to cool on both sides.

Meanwhile, Secretary MacDonald moved to rebuild public confidence in WSDOT's ability to deliver projects on time and on budget. He directed WSDOT divisions and programs to establish quantifiable benchmarks for monitoring their performance on the principle, "What gets measured, gets managed." Departmental performance vis-a-vis these milestones would be publicized via regular reports to the Legislature, to the public, and on the WSDOT website.

Then, on September 11, 2001, Al Qaeda terrorists launched their deadly attacks against New York City and Washington, D.C. The world recoiled in horror, and America's transportation system screeched to a temporary halt. Safeguarding key state transportation assets and services, notably ferries, became a major new responsibility for WSDOT.

Stabilizing the Alaskan Way Viaduct after the 2001 earthquake.

A New Hand on the Wheel

Douglas B. MacDonald's appointment as Washington's fourth Secretary of Transportation included a personal dividend — the return to the state in which he grew up, after 38 years studying and living elsewhere. After graduating in 1963 from Mercer Island High School, MacDonald went to college in Boston, did a stint in the Peace Corps in Africa, took a law degree in Boston, and joined a law firm in Chicago. He returned to Boston for his first public sector management assignment, serving as Chief Legal Counsel from 1975 to 1981 for the Massachusetts Port Authority. The next 11 years were spent with a Boston law firm.

In 1992, MacDonald was named Executive Director of the Massachusetts Water Resources Authority, responsible for drinking water supply and wastewater treatment for 60 Boston-area communities. Over nine years, he guided the on time and on budget delivery of the $4 billion construction program for new wastewater facilities for the nationally recognized clean-up of Boston Harbor and laid the groundwork for $2 billion of modernization facilities for drinking water supply systems. His reputation for hands-on management and a passion for public accountability led to his recruitment and appointment by the Washington State Transportation Commission. He joined WSDOT in April 2001.

A long list of unfunded transportation needs across the state met MacDonald as incoming secretary. But the immediate challenge was public and legislative skepticism about WSDOT's capabilities and performance. Accountability and project delivery became WSDOT's new watchwords — working with public officials, local governments, citizens, contractors, WSDOT's own employees, and the press — in order to forge the restoration of public confidence that would be critical to the Legislature's willingness to lead the way to fresh funding initiatives for transportation needs in every corner of the state.

Under MacDonald, WSDOT has seized new opportunities in project engineering, construction contracting, traffic incident management, intergovernmental cooperation, and public information — its website for traveler information and program accountability is recognized as among the tops in the country — and in environmental protection. Today, with significant new funding commitments in hand, MacDonald's challenge continues in accountability and project delivery: Help WSDOT make every dollar count.

New Map, Old Road

In January 2002, the Legislature focused anew on the prescriptions and proposals offered by the Blue Ribbon Commission's 2000 report. As member (now State Transportation Commission chair) Dale Stedman later recalled, "The first step was to address the widespread public perception that WSDOT had enough money to meet the state's needs if it was just more efficient." The commission and department also had to combat many public myths such as the idea that rural-area gas taxes subsidize urban projects. In fact, metropolitan revenues underwrite services and improvements in the less populated counties.

To help rebuild public confidence, the 2002 Legislature adopted a "transportation efficiencies" bill based on Blue Ribbon recommendations. The department also began planning a major "reduction in force" to trim more than 500 positions in case funding failed to materialize for new projects.

In spring 2002, Doug MacDonald reached out to the public via radio talk shows and the news media while WSDOT launched publication of quarterly "Gray Notebooks" detailing the Department's performance by "Measures, Markers and Mileposts." Newspapers across the state praised WSDOT's new candor, and the *Puget Sound Business Journal* found the Gray Notebook's detail to be "addictive."

On the anniversary of his appointment, Doug MacDonald wrote WSDOT employees, "Not in my wildest dreams could I have foreseen all the things that would happen at WSDOT this year. Every corner of the agency has made its contributions. Countless individuals have gone beyond the call of duty." He was proudest

The 9/11 attacks delayed the first "Fruit Express" shipment. Below: Incident Response Team vehicle.

of "the improvement both for WSDOT and the Transportation Commission in communicating about our activities." MacDonald believed "We have entered a much more constructive relationship with the legislature in helping to steer the future policy directions in our state."

Such positive change would be needed to bridge the growing gap between Washington's transportation revenues and needs. The state's rate of transportation capital investment had essentially remained flat since 1980 while everything else had increased dramatically: population up 43 percent, employment up 58 percent, vehicle registrations up 57 percent, ferry patronage up 59 percent, and vehicle miles traveled up a whopping 88 percent. The aging of the interstate highway system and other infrastructure and mounting peak-hour congestion in major corridors made new investment all the more urgent.

Governor Locke pressed for a scaled-back version of his 2001 plan and expected success now that Democrats had reclaimed control of the House. However, Speaker Frank Chopp feared that direct passage of a major gas-tax increase would backfire in the November elections and refuel the anti-tax bandwagon.

Ultimately, the Legislature drafted an awkward compromise with two main elements: Referendum 51 for a nine-cent

Douglas MacDonald becomes fourth Secretary of Transportation on April 23, 2001.

Construction of first segment of US 395 "North Spokane Corridor" project begins on August 22, 2001.

Terrorist attacks temporarily shut down many transportation systems on September 11, 2001, and lead to intensified security precautions for airports, ferries, railroads, and highways.

The Washington Fruit Express rail service is inaugurated on September 17, 2001.

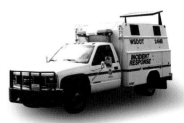

Timeline

Enhancing freight mobility has become a top priority in the I-5 corridor. Below: Searching for ancient human remains at Port Angeles graving dock site before it was abandoned in 2004.

Washington's first HOV lane outside the Puget Sound region opens on I-5 in Vancouver on October 29, 2001.

WSDOT issues Freight Implementation Plan in November 2002.

Washington voters reject Referendum 51 transportation plan and gas-tax increase while approving Initiative 776, which seeks to cap local MVET surcharges, on November 5, 2002. Seattle voters narrowly approve and fund a new Seattle Popular Monorail Authority to construct a 14-mile "Green Line" system.

gas-tax increase and other fee hikes to fund a relatively detailed transportation plan, and a new "Regional Transportation Investment District," or RTID, to raise regional revenue to meet Puget Sound's special (and especially expensive) needs. These included replacing the SR 520 floating bridge and Seattle's Alaskan Way Viaduct, both of which were vulnerable in the event of the next major earthquake.

Referendum 51 promised $7.8 billion over the coming decade for transportation improvements. Although most major business and labor interests rallied behind R-51, some environmental and pro-transit constituencies in metropolitan Puget Sound felt the plan was tilted too heavily toward highways. With the Republican Party officially neutral and anti-tax forces energized by Initiative 776, Tim Eyman's latest attack on motor vehicle excise taxes, the lack of urban progressive enthusiasm for R 51 would prove fatal.

Referendum 51 was turned down by 62 percent of the

electorate on November 5, 2002. The message for WSDOT was crystal clear: Much remained to be done in building public confidence in the state's ability to deliver projects and to account to citizens for the return of value on new tax dollars. Despite this skepticism, Initiative 776 barely survived the election, and its main goal of repealing Sound Transit's special MVET revenues was repudiated by Sound Transit district voters and later blocked by the State Supreme Court. An even tighter majority in Seattle — just 877 votes to be precise — approved $1.7 billion in new MVET taxes to build a new "Green Line" monorail system.

Back to the Drawing Board

WSDOT wasted no time mourning R-51. MacDonald, other WSDOT staff, and Transportation Commissioners crisscrossed the state offering "straight talk about transportation" both to detail the challenges and to publicize WSDOT's progress. The latter included dramatic improvements in project delivery performance, more effective cost management for main-

THE COMMISSIONER

Aubrey Davis Jr. has played one role or another in shaping Washington's transportation system since 1968, when he campaigned for King County's "Forward Thrust" mass transit plan. His large collection of "hats" includes Mayor of Mercer Island, chair of King County Metro's Transportation Committee, regional representative of the U.S. Secretary of Transportation, regional administrator of the Federal Transit Administration, chair of the Sound Transit expert review committee and of the Governor's task force on the 1990 sinking of the Lake Washington Floating Bridge, and member and three-time chair of the Washington State Transportation Commission between 1992 and 2004.

Davis led the successful campaign to create the Metro Transit (now part of King County) regional bus system in 1972, but he is perhaps best known for helping to broker the redesign of Interstate 90, which would have cut a wide trench through central Seattle and Mercer Island. In 1974, he joined with other local officials and Highway Department leaders to devise the "3-2T-3" compromise incorporating dedicated transit lanes and extensive lidding and landscaping in Seattle and Mercer Island. He was also Governor Dixy Lee Ray's first choice to serve as Secretary of the new Department of Transportation in 1977.

Born in Pasadena in 1917, Davis took his degree in political science at Occidental College and earned a Washington, D.C., internship in the first federal public housing programs in 1939. After his Army tour of duty during World War II, Davis rejoined the Federal Public Housing Administration and was assigned to Seattle with his wife, Henrietta. He helped organize local wage stabilization programs during the Korean War and volunteered at Group Health Cooperative (whose board he later chaired).

Davis left the federal employ in 1954 and ultimately helped to establish and chair Gaco Western, Inc., a successful manufacturer of industrial and residential coating products. He was elected to the Mercer Island City Council in 1967 just as the first plans for I-90 were being unveiled, which put him on a new career track that has lasted nearly 40 years. Davis also chairs Coastal Environmental Systems, a designer and manufacturer of weather and environmental monitoring systems.

Tacoma Link (Sound Transit).

tenance programs, new business practices for Washington State Ferries, innovations in commuter travel information systems, and growing praise for WSDOT's accountability initiatives such as the quarterly Gray Notebook performance reports.

The 2003 session of the Legislature offered some hope for progress. New House Transportation Chair Ed Murray, who had succeeded Ruth Fisher upon her retirement (she joined the Transportation Commission in 2004 but died soon after), advocated a modest three-cent gas-tax increase and other fee hikes, but legislators were gun shy after R 51's defeat, and MVET was effectively off the table except for local option projects.

Thanks to the reforms underway in the department, legislative criticisms of its performance and efficiency became less shrill. With the leadership of the Legislative Transportation Committee, both houses of the Legislature arrived at a new compromise: a "temporary" five-cent gas-tax increase to raise $4.5 billion over a decade for a prescribed list of "priority projects" selected by it. Democrats and Republicans negotiated a fragile political ceasefire to allow legislators of both parties to support the "nickel tax," to prevent it from becoming an issue in future elections. Most of the public accepted the gas-tax increase, the first since 1991, even though it coincided with a spike in pump prices spurred by the Iraq War and market factors.

The Legislature also approved a 0.3 percent sales tax on new and used vehicles to fund a "Multi-modal Transportation Account" chiefly to benefit transit agencies and passenger ferry service, and it implemented another Blue Ribbon Commission proposal by creating an independent Transportation Performance Audit Board to monitor WSDOT reforms and programs.

The department recognized that the "nickel projects" posed both a technical and a political challenge. They put WSDOT in the spotlight to prove it could deliver the goods on time and on budget. The department's public information and reporting systems were reorganized accordingly to detail its progress — or shortcomings — for each and every funded project.

Secretary MacDonald issues Executive Order 1025 directing closer consultation and cooperation with Indian tribes on February 19, 2003.

The United States and its allies attack Iraq on March 20, 2003, resulting in military duty for hundreds of WSDOT employees.

Five-cent-per-gallon gas-tax increase takes effect on July 1, 2003, to fund $4.5 billion in priority "nickel projects."

Vintage Yakima Valley car (YVTC).

Modern road work, clockwise: Monitoring I-5 traffic, GPS survey crew, paving with recycled surfacing, testing samples in the laboratory.

MAKING HIGHWAYS SMARTER

Washington's leadership in transportation research and engineering dates back to 1921, when it established the predecessor of today's Materials Testing Laboratory in the basement of the Supreme Court. This unit

now ensures that materials used by contractors meet specifications, evaluates the geological and structural stability of planned projects and sites, and tests soils and pavements in the field.

WSDOT has been a national pioneer in the use of "dowel bars" to extend the life of concrete joints and in the design of a computerized "Pavement Management System" to program the most efficient maintenance and replacement of highways. WSDOT's regional offices have introduced novel solutions such as lane-edge "rumble strips," de-icing systems for bridges, and aerodynamic vanes to control snow drifts. Not every innovation works — there was an unfortunate experience using recycled tires for fill in 1996 — but as former laboratory manager Denny Jackson notes, "That's how you learn."

Since the initial installation of ramp meters in 1981, WSDOT has expanded its use of Intelligent Transportation Systems (ITS) with continued expansion of ramp meters and installation of closed-circuit TV cameras and variable message signs mounted over the freeway lanes on the Puget Sound freeway system. Cameras have also been installed in heavily traveled corridors providing real-time images of traffic and weather conditions via the department's website.

Beginning in 2001 these ITS devices became part of a new emphasis on operating the highway system to its maximum efficiency in addition to constructing new capacity. WSDOT reorganized its Maintenance and Operations Division to lead this new mission. This entailed a major expansion of the incident response program in cooperation with the Washington State Patrol with the goal of clearing highway accidents and obstructions within 90 minutes. The WSDOT website was enhanced to provide real-time travel and weather information that also allows motorists to calculate their commute time in major Puget Sound freeway corridors before leaving the home or office. WSDOT camera-feeds and traffic data are used widely by the news media and by wireless services for devices such as the handheld "Traffic Gauge," so drivers aren't caught by surprise on the road. The department also participates in the national 511 traffic info hotline.

Working on the new Tacoma Narrows Bridge in 2004. Right: Rush hour traffic on Bellevue's I-405 (Nick Gunderson).

Another transportation milestone was reached on August 22, 2003, when Puget Sound's first new streetcars in six decades rolled down Tacoma's Pacific Avenue. Although only a short 1.6-mile line, the new "Link" service connected with an intermodal terminal for Sound Transit Regional Express buses, local transit, and "Sounder" commuter rail, and thereby gave commuters a ticket to ride all the way to Seattle — something people used to do every day a century ago.

Concern for the economic consequences of statewide and regional transportation shortcomings became critical in the fall of 2003 as Washington competed with other states for selection to assemble Boeing's new 7E7 (now 787) Dreamliner. Boeing had already shocked the local community by abruptly shifting its corporate headquarters from Seattle to Chicago in 2001. Now it might take a big chunk of its capital investment and payroll elsewhere.

Boeing Commercial Airplanes CEO Alan Mulally publicly criticized Washington's business climate and singled out lack of investment in the state's transportation system as a major stumbling block in Washington's prospects for the 7E7 project. Behind the scenes, the company had already advised the Legislature that Washington would not even make the "short list" if the nickel tax plan failed.

The State did ultimately prevail on December 15, 2003, but only after promising more than $3 billion in tax breaks and subsidies, including major highway improvements included in the nickel tax program to serve Boeing's Everett facilities.

The Road Ahead

WSDOT made good progress on its "nickel projects" in 2004, and bids came in almost precisely on the department's estimates of $3.11 billion. Work also advanced on the new Tacoma Narrows Bridge, which survived a local referendum on planned tolls, and was 56 percent complete by the end of 2004.

The news was not so good for one of the department's high-priority projects: replacement of the eastern half of the Hood Canal Floating Bridge's aging pontoons. WSDOT had broken ground for a needed drydock near Port Angeles in August 2003, but work halted almost immediately with the discovery of ancient Native American remains. After consultation with tribal leaders, scientists, and elected officials, WSDOT formally abandoned the site in December 2004.

Planning for the new Regional Transportation Investment District also stalled as local leaders tried to prioritize competing needs. Looming over the discussion was the massive expense of replacing Seattle's precarious Alaskan Way Viaduct. On this project at least, the City of Seattle and WSDOT could agree: A tunnel was selected as the best option in December 2004, but meeting its potential $4 billion cost would require more discussion and ultimate public assent.

First Asian American WSTC member Chris Marr. Below: Governor Christine Gregoire.

Ground is broken for Hood Canal Bridge East Half Replacement Project on August 6, 2003.

Sound Transit's Tacoma Link, the state's first modern light rail system, makes its inaugural run on August 22, 2003.

WSF discontinues passenger-only ferry service between Seattle and Bremerton on September 20, 2003, due to lack of funds.

Boeing announces that it will assemble its new 7E7 (787) Dreamliner in Everett on December 15, 2003.

Skagit Transportation Center opens in downtown Mount Vernon in January 2004.

In 2004, the effects of the department's reforms and new practices became apparent. New Incident Response Teams quickly restored traffic flows after highway accidents. New environmental policies curbed herbicide use, restored long dead salmon streams, and integrated habitat protection into project design. Engineers demonstrated

innovative techniques for bridge construction, extending pavement life, and controlling snow and ice. New laws, aggressive enforcement, and education efforts by a variety of agencies dramatically reduced traffic fatalities. Most importantly, all but a few nickel projects advanced toward completion on schedule and on budget.

Against this background, business, labor, and environmental leaders from around the state formed a "Transportation Partnership" to lobby for new funding. In January 2005, the Legislature convened in Olympia. The previous November's

Rep. Helen Sommers, Sen. Mary Margaret Haugen, Rep. Ed Murray, and Rep. Fred Jarrett celebrate passage of 2005 transportation plan.

extraordinarily close and bitterly contested election of Democratic State Attorney General Christine Gregoire as governor over Republican State Senator Dino Rossi hung over the new session, dimming hopes for any significant bipartisan agreement on reform or investment in transportation.

Despite precarious Democratic majorities in both chambers, House Transportation Chair Ed Murray of Seattle and Senate Transportation Chair Mary Margaret Haugen of Camano Island pressed for ambitious packages. They also won qualified support from Republican leaders such as Representative Beverly Woods and Senator Dan Swecker.

In mid-April each house passed major plans chiefly funded through phased increases in the gas tax. A "conference committee" representing both houses of the Legislature then met to reconcile the two bills. In the final days of the session, the committee unveiled a compromise costing $8.5 billion — the largest single program ever contemplated for transportation in Washington. It would be chiefly funded by a 9.5-cent increase in the gas tax phased in over four years along with other

MEASURING UP

Since spring 2002, the Washington State Department of Transportation has published a quarterly overview of its performance formally titled "Measures, Markers and Mileposts," but better known as the "Gray Notebook" for its cover. The report offers detailed data on projects, maintenance, operations, budgets and spending, schedules, and other indicators of departmental progress — or shortcomings. Praised by citizens, elected officials, and the news media for its scope and candor, the Gray Notebook is also available online at www.wsdot.wa.gov along with a condensed "lite" version.

fees. Nearly half of the funding targeted replacement of "at-risk" structures such as the Alaskan Way Viaduct and the SR 520 floating bridge and expansion of I-405 — augmented by another $3 billion-plus to be raised in the region.

The conference report passed the Senate with respectable bipartisan support but failed in the House. Governor Gregoire and leaders on both sides of the aisle hammered out solutions to legislators' concerns and the "Transportation Partnership Investment Fund" (Engrossed Senate Substitue Bill 6103) won passage on reconsideration just hours before the House adjourned at 7:17 p.m., on Sunday, April 24. Companion legislation shifted authority for appointing and overseeing the Secretary of Transportation from the Transportation Commission to the governor. The Transportation Commission was retained and independent auditing of the department's performance was strengthened.

The day after the legislature adjourned, Secretary MacDonald advised his employees to "buckle your seatbelts."

Thus, 100 years and one week after the the original State Highway Board held its first meeting on April 17, 1905, one chapter in the history of the Washington State Department of Transportation closed and another opened.

The restored original 1908 Colman Dock tower clock, which was reinstalled in 2005.

Sound Transit and WSDOT open new I-405 HOV ramps in downtown Bellevue on November 16, 2004.

WSDOT and City of Seattle select tunnel design as the preferred alternative to replace Seattle's Alaskan Way Viaduct on December 7, 2004.

WSDOT abandons Hood Canal Floating Bridge pontoon construction dry dock site near Port Angeles to protect Native American remains on December 21, 2004.

W. Michael Anderson is named director of Washington State Ferries on February 25, 2005.

The 100th anniversary of the creation of the State Highway Board is observed with a ceremony in the State Capitol on March 15, 2005.

Legislature approves $8.5 billion Transportation Partnership Investment Fund on April 24, 2005.

Governor Christine Gregoire signs TPIF and other tranportation reforms on May 9, 2005.

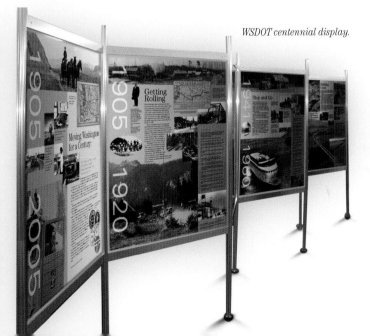

WSDOT centennial display.

Appendix 1

WASHINGTON STATE TRANSPORTATION COMMISSION, 2005

Dale Stedman, Chair
Dan O'Neal, Vice-chair
Ed Barnes
Robert Distler
Richard Ford
Elmira Forner
Michele Maher

WSDOT EXECUTIVE MANAGEMENT TEAM, 2005

Douglas B. MacDonald, Secretary of Transportation
Paula J. Hammond, Chief of Staff
John F. Conrad, Assistant Secretary for Engineering and Regional Operations
Richard Ybarra, Assistant Secretary for Finance & Administration
Michael Anderson, Executive Director for Washington State Ferries
Don Nelson, Director, Environmental & Engineering Programs
Gummada Murthy, Director for Maintenance & Operations Programs
Jerry Lenzi, Region Administrator, Eastern Region (Spokane)
Don Senn, Region Administrator, North Central Region (Wenatchee)
Lorena Eng, Region Administrator, Northwest Region (Seattle)
Randy Hain, Region Administrator, Olympic Region (Tumwater)
Don Whitehouse, Region Administrator, South Central Region (Yakima)
Don Wagner, Region Administrator, Southwest Region (Vancouver)
David Dye, Administrator, Urban Corridors Office
John Sibold, Director, Aviation Division
Kathleen Davis, Director, Highways & Local Programs
Amy Arnis, Deputy Director, Strategic Planning & Programming
Judy Giniger, Director, Public Transportation & Rail
Jerry A. Ellis, Director, Transportation Economic Partnerships
Barbara Ivanov, Director, Freight Strategy & Policy
Steve McKerney, Director, Internal Audits
Brenda Nnambi, Director, Equal Opportunity Office
Debra Gregory, Ombudsman
Colleen Jollie, Tribal Liaison
Linda Mullen, Director, Communications Office
Larry Ehl, Federal Legislative Liaison
Don Griffith, State Legislative Liaison

Appendix 2

WSDOT CENTENNIAL PLANNING STEERING COMMITTEE, 2004–2005

Stan Moon, CH2M Hill
(WSDOT retired), Co-chair

Dennis Jackson, KBI, Inc. (WSDOT retired),
Co-chair

Paula J. Hammond,
WSDOT Chief of Staff

John F. Conrad, WSDOT Assistant Secretary
for Engineering &
Regional Operations

Debra L. Gregory, Special Assistant
for Policy & Administration

Aubrey Davis, Washington State
Transportation Commission (retired)

Janet Ray, AAA of Washington

Connie Rus, WSDOT Graphics
Communications Manager

DawnMarie Moe,
WSDOT Interactive Communications

Joyce Norris,
WSDOT Executive Assistant

Shannon Gordon,
WSDOT Public Information Officer

Marilyn Bowman,
WSDOT Administrative Services Manager

Jennifer Ziegler, Transportation Commission
Administrator

Walt Crowley, HistoryLink Liaison

Appendix 3

WASHINGTON STATE'S TRANSPORTATION CHIEF EXECUTIVES, 1905–2005

Highway Commissioners, 1905–1923

Joseph M. Snow, 1905–1909
Henry L. Bowlby, 1909–1911
William J. Roberts, 1911–1913
William R. Roy, 1913–1916
James Allen, 1916–1923

Highway Engineers, 1923–1929

James Allen, 1923–1925
J. W. Hoover, 1925–1927
Samuel J. Humes, 1927–1929

Directors of Highways, 1929–1977

Samuel J. Humes, 1929–1933
Lacey V. Murrow, 1933–1940
Burwell Bantz, 1941–1945
Clarence Shain, 1945–1949
William A. Bugge, 1949–1963
Charles G. Prahl, 1963–1969
George H. Andrews, 1969–1975
William A. Bulley, 1975–1977

Secretaries of Transportation, 1977–2005

William A. Bulley, 1977–1981

Duane Berentson, 1981–1993

Sid Morrison, 1993–2001

Douglas B. MacDonald, 2001–

Appendix 4

MEMBERS OF THE WASHINGTON STATE HIGHWAY COMMISSION, 1951–1977, AND WASHINGTON STATE TRANSPORTATION COMMISSION, 1977–2005

(In chronological order of appointment with hometowns and party affiliations; *denotes chairs)

George B. Simpson, 1951–54, Vancouver, D
John E. Maley, 1951, Omak
Fred G. Redmon,* 1951–54, Yakima, R
R. A. Moisio,* 1951–61, Tacoma
Oscar E. Stone, 1951–61, Spokane
L. B. Wallace, 1951–54, Bellingham
R. E. Hensel, 1954–57, Bremerton
Ernest C. Huntley,* 1954–57, Colfax
Harry E. Morgan, 1954–61,
Longview & Ocean Park
Ernest A. Cowell,* 1957–65, Eureka, D
Ernest J. Ketcham,* 1957–63, Seattle
George D. Zahn,* 1961–71, Methow, D
James M. Blair Sr., 1961–67, Puyallup, D
Robert L. Mikalson, 1961–71, Centralia, D
Irving Clark Jr., 1963–65, Seattle, D
Harold Walsh, 1965–74, Everett, D
Elmer C. Huntley,* 1965–67, Thornton, R
Baker Ferguson,* 1967–76, Walla Walla, R
John N. Rupp,* 1967–73, Seattle, R
Lorna Ream, 1971–73, 1976–77 Spokane
A. H. Parker,* 1971–76 Bremerton, R

(Note: Transportation Commission succeeded Highway Commission in 1977)

Virginia K. Gunby, 1973–79, Seattle, D
Howard Sorensen,* 1973–77, Ellensburg, R
Julia Butler Hansen,* 1975–80, Cathlamet, D
Ray A. Aardal,* 1977–81, Bremerton, D
James G. Swinyard, 1977–81, Deer Park, R
Robert L. Mikalson, 1977–83, Centralia, D

Vaughn Hubbard,* 1977–89, Waitsburg, R
Richard Odabashian,* 1978–91, Cashmere, R
Gov. Albert D. Rosellini,* 1979–91, Seattle, D
Jerry B. Overton,* 1981–87, Spokane, R
F. "Pat" Wanamaker,* 1981–86, Coupeville, R
Bernice Stern,* 1981–91, Seattle, D
Leo B. Sweeney,* 1983–93, Olympia, D
William J. Kamps,* 1986–90, Bremerton, D
Jim Henning,* 1987–94, St. John, R
Norm McKibben,* 1989–93, Walla Walla, R
Alice B. Tawresey,* 1990–98, Bainbridge Is., R
Robert M. Higgins, 1991–93, Spokane, D
Barbara Shinpoch, 1991–93, Renton, D
Aubrey Davis Jr.,* 1992–2004,
Mercer Island, D
Connie Niva,* 1993–2003, Everett, D
Lawrence Weldon, 1993–94, Seattle, D
Linda Tompkins,* 1993–97, Spokane, D
Dick Thompson, 1994–96, Ellensburg, R
Pat Patterson, 1994–97, Pullman, R
Ed Barnes, 1995–, Vancouver, D
Tom Green,* 1996–99, Wenatchee, R
A. Michèle Maher, 1997–, Spokane, R
Christopher Marr,* 1997–2003, Spokane, D
George Kargianis, 1998–2004, Bellevue, R
Elmira Forner, 2000–, Manson, R
Dale Stedman,* 2003–, Spokane, R
Dan O'Neal, 2003–, Belfair, D
Ruth Fisher, 2004–05, Tacoma, D
Dick Ford, 2004–, Seattle, D
Robert Distler, 2005–, Orcas Island, D

Appendix 5

WASHINGTON STATE TRANSPORTATION EMPLOYEES KILLED ON DUTY,

1950–2005

Frank E. Potter, December 1, 1950

Laird D. Chambers, December 15, 1950

Charles P. Getty, January 23, 1951

L. A. Parton, February 13, 1951

Richard I. Temple, March 30, 1951

William R. Pitts, August 20, 1951

Rollow S. Clark, November 20, 1951

Ray Wittig, February 4, 1952

Paul J. Yandt, July 29, 1953

Joseph F. Franz, September 21, 1953

Henry D. Willis, April 16, 1954

Fred G. Tegtmeier, March 7, 1955

Edward Bowles, July 5, 1955

Albert E. Holman, September 19, 1956

Andrew Kaelberer, December 27, 1956

Lucien L. Houston, February 22, 1957

Knute Johnson, October 4, 1957

Clarence R. Sluder, October 4, 1957

Harrell J. Shull, April 29, 1959

Francis E. Baker, May 8, 1959

George H. Mulfinger, May 8, 1959

James P. O'Neil, January 27, 1960

William F. Holmes, June 14, 1960

Eino Mattila, December 12, 1962

Vernon E. Curtis, March 20, 1963

Gary Davis, December 11, 1963

Lee W. Robinson, October 30, 1964

Charles O. Williams, February 2, 1965

Claude M. Waterman, June 18, 1966

George J. Heaton, June 18, 1966

Wallace D. Wright, October 22, 1966

Harold J. Allen, June 30, 1967

Donald G. Barden, November 20, 1969

Ray T. Collie, February 28, 1970

William T. Owens, June 15, 1971

Harold L. Gustafson, August 31, 1973

William L. Ashley, August 3, 1976

William L. Cook, May 24, 1977

Edward N. Abrams, September 9, 1977

George D. Adair, December 5, 1979

Russell H. Barker, December 14, 1979

Dermot R. Moore, January 21, 1980

James C. Wishard, May 19, 1980

Robert N. Johnson, February 14, 1982

Robert J. Forrest, July 7, 1982

Richard L. Androsko, August 28, 1984

Joseph C. Craig, October 11, 1985

John D. Swan, October 11, 1985

Loren L. Wharton, February 8, 1988

Patricia L. Oberg, July 19, 1989

Donald E. Fritsvold, August 21, 1991

Gordon J. Burlingame, July 17, 1992

Michael D. Malone, June 4, 1993

Edward J. Fabeck, October 6, 1994

Samuel E. Williams, February 22, 2000

Wayne "Jake" Boardson, August 12, 2002

Appendix 6

SELECTED DEPARTMENTAL AND PROJECT AWARDS

1964

- Washington State Department of Highways: Greatest Improvement in Traffic Safety, Western Insurance Information Service.

1967

- Stillaguamish Bridge on SR 530 near Cicero: National Award for Esthetic Design, Safety and Utility, American Institute of Steel Construction.

1968

- Toutle River Bridge on I–5 north of Castle Rock: Progress in Engineering Design of Arc-Welded Structures, Lincoln Foundation.
- North Fork Stillaguamish River Bridge: Most Beautiful Steel Bridge, Short Span, American Institute of Steel Construction.
- 24 mile section of I-90 between Cle Elum and Ellensburg: America's Safest and Most Beautiful Highway, Special Mention, *PARADE* Magazine.
- Satsop River Bridge: National First Prize for Beauty, Short Span, American Institute of Steel Construction.

1970

- Urban Plaza and Fountain at Sixth Avenue and Seneca Street (part of Seattle I-5 Freeway): Excellence in Highway Beautification, U.S. Department of Transportation.

1978

- Ed Hendler Intercity Bridge, Pasco: Presidential Design Award, Federal Highway Administration (FHWA).

1990

- Capitol Boulevard Bridge Replacement, I-5 in Olympia: Excellence in Highway Design, Award of Excellence, FHWA.
- Washington State Convention & Trade Center Lid over I-5, Seattle: Excellence in Highway Design, Award of Excellence, FHWA.
- Mt. Baker Ridge Tunnel and I-90 Lid, Seattle: Outstanding Engineering Achievement, American Society of Landscape Architects.
- SR 410 (Highway Improvements on Federally Owned Lands): Excellence in Highway Design, Award of Excellence, FHWA.

1994

- I-90 Pedestrian/Bicycle Trail, Seattle to Bellevue: Excellence in Highway Design, Award of Merit, FHWA.
- I-5 Freeway Landscaping, Olympia: Excellence in Highway Design, Award of Merit, FHWA.

1999

- I-5/South Dupont Interchange: National Quality Initiative Achievement Award, State Winner, FHWA.

2000

- Advanced Environmental Mitigation Revolving Account: Best Practices in Environmental Partnering, American Association of State Highway and Transportation Officials (AASHTO).

2001
- Alternative Mitigation Policy Guidance: Best Practices in Environmental Partnering, AASHTO.
- Intersection Safety Improvement Priority Program: Safety Award, FHWA, 2001.

2002
- Twisp River Bridge: Design Award for Excellence, Precast/Prestressed Concrete Institute.
- Transportation Commissioner Connie Niva: HOV Leadership Award, International High Occupancy Vehicle Conference.
- First Creek Fish Passage Project on Lake Chelan: Excellence in Highway Design, Award of Excellence, FHWA.

2003
- Transportation Demand Management Resource Center, Urban Planning Office, National Leadership Award, Association for Commuter Transportation.
- WSDOT Pavement Guide — Interactive (Linda Pierce, Steve Muench, Joe Mahoney): National Premier Award, National Engineering Educational Delivery System.
- WSDOT Traffic Information website: National Award for Traveler Information Web Sites, FHWA.

- Roadside Classification Plan and Roadside Manual: Environmental Excellence Award for Roadside Resource Management and Maintenance, FHWA.

2004
- SR 90 and SR 519 Intermodal Access Phase 1: Excellence in Highway Design, Award of Merit, FHWA.

Appendix 7

BLUE RIBBON COMMISSION ON TRANSPORTATION RECOMMENDATIONS, 2000

The final report of the Blue Ribbon Commission on Transportation laid out 18 detailed recommendations to reorganize, finance, and guide the future of transportation. While long-term funding remains unresolved and some reforms were rejected, most of the Commission's proposals have been implemented by legislative or administrative action, especially to enhance agency accountability. The Commission's final recommendations are listed below in their original language (with comment as appropriate):

1. Adopt transportation benchmarks as a cornerstone of government accountability at the state, city, county, and transit district levels.

2. Establish a single point of accountability at the state level strengthening the role of the state in ensuring the accountability of the statewide transportation system.

3. Direct a thorough and independent performance review of WSDOT administration practices and staffing levels.

4. Remove the barriers to achieving the transportation benchmarks for efficiency and system performance. Provide funding for a strong state and regional transportation system.

5. Invest in maintenance, preservation, and improvement of the entire transportation system so that the transportation benchmarks can be achieved.

6. Provide regions with the ability to plan, select, fund, and implement (or contract implementation of) projects identified to meet the region's transportation and land use goals.

7. Achieve construction and project delivery efficiencies.

8. Incorporate the design-build process and its variations into construction projects to achieve the goals of time savings and avoidance of costly change orders.

9. Use the private sector to deliver projects and transportation services.

10. Re-engineer the workplace to achieve greater efficiency, and consider the use of managed competition for operations and maintenance functions.

11. Streamline permitting processes for transportation projects.

12. Link transportation funding to efficiencies.

13. Link maintenance and preservation funds to best practices.

14. Simplify funding distributions for best results.

Appendix 8

PHOTO NOTES AND CREDITS

15. Allow regions to retain funds they raise.

16. Seek a 90 percent fare box recovery for ferry system operational costs within 20 years.

17. Develop a package of new revenues to fund a comprehensive multi-modal set of investments, which, taken together with the recommended efficiency measures and reforms, will ensure a 20-year program of preserving, optimizing, and expanding the state's transportation system. (The BRCT outlined $150 billion in total needs over 20 years. Subtracting projected revenues from existing sources and potential efficiency savings, it identified a revenue shortfall of between $30 billion and $40 billion, including the costs of the Early Action Plan described below.)

18. Begin action now to improve the transportation system, guided by the BRCT Early Action Plan. (This plan itemized a set of urgent projects and actions estimated to cost between $9.6 billion and $12.7 billion over six years.)

Key to Cover Photo Gallery of Selected Washington State Transportation Leaders: From left to right, Ruth Fisher, Lacey V. Murrow, Fred Redmon, Julia Butler Hansen, Aubrey Davis Jr., William A. Bugge, Charles G. Prahl, George H. Andrews, Duane Berentson, Sid Morrison, Connie Niva, Douglas B. MacDonald, and William A. Bulley.

Inside Front Cover: Original Lake Washington Floating Bridge Mount Baker Tunnel entrance, Seattle, 1940 (WSDOT Archives)

Inside Back Cover: Skykomish River Bridge, Stevens Pass Highway (US 2), mid-1930s (WSDOT Archives)

All photographs in this book were provided by Paul Dorpat, History Ink, or WSDOT unless otherwise noted. Some photos may also reside in other institutional collections.

Special thanks to University of Washington Libraries Special Collections; Jeremiah Coughlan, *The Columbian*, Vancouver; Tom Suarez, Sound Transit; Nick Gunderson; and Mark Bozanich, www.angelfire.com/wa2/hwysofwastate/, for selected images.